IMPARTIAL

A Journey through The Acts of the Apostles 1-10

AUDREY LUPISELLA

WESTBOW
PRESS®
A DIVISION OF THOMAS NELSON
& ZONDERVAN

WestBow Press books may be ordered through booksellers or by contacting:

WestBow Press
A Division of Thomas Nelson & Zondervan
1663 Liberty Drive
Bloomington, IN 47403
www.westbowpress.com
1 (866) 928-1240

Scripture quotations are from the ESV® Bible (The Holy Bible, English
Standard Version®), copyright © 2001 by Crossway, a publishing ministry
of Good News Publishers. Used by permission. All rights reserved.

ISBN: 978-1-5127-6841-1 (sc)
ISBN: 978-1-5127-6842-8 (hc)
ISBN: 978-1-5127-6840-4 (e)

Library of Congress Control Number: 2016920513

Print information available on the last page.

WestBow Press rev. date: 12/30/2016

Contents

Introduction

Hello, beloved! How I praise God for you—how you are seeking to know Him and deepen your relationship with your Savior. I have been a Christian for most of my life, but I haven't always lived as a Christian should. I grew up in church, did confirmation in fifth grade, and was baptized in my preacher's backyard pool. But sometime in middle school, things went very wayward. I became hard and rebellious. I took all the anger that was inside me out on my family and decided that God had never done me any favors. Why should I listen to Him?

I kept going farther and farther down the wrong path, despite the numerous signs and warnings given by God. Eventually, I got pregnant at sixteen years of age. I had a beautiful baby boy and had to grow up and take care of him before I even knew how to take care of myself. However, I still did not turn to God. I chose to be a single mother and put myself through college "all on my own."

Driven by pride, I went straight off a cliff. It was many more years filled with many more mistakes before I finally shattered. I hit rock bottom and simply could not put myself back together. During this time, I kept hearing the words of Psalm 6:2–3 running through my brain: "My bones are in agony. My soul is in deep anguish. How long, Lord? How long?"

I finally cried these words of the psalmist out to Go. I just could not take it anymore. I could not hold up under the stress and the heartbreak. It took someone more than me to put me back together. It took my Creator, my Savior. I just had to give myself over to Him let Him stitch me back together, and let Him fill me with His peace, His joy, His strength, and His endurance.

For the next six years, I felt like God had placed a specific calling on my life, but for the life of me, I had no idea what it was. I prayed and prayed and prayed. I graduated with a bachelor's degree in exercise science, had a great career in the fitness industry, and married an amazing man.

Finally, after six years of praying and waiting, God spoke to me. I was driving to work, and I audibly heard Him tell me to go to seminary. So I did! Within two months, I was enrolled in seminary. I was studying toward a master's degree in biblical studies and had absolutely no idea what I was going to do with it. People thought I was plain crazy. Half the time, I thought I was crazy!

God proved Himself faithful, as He is wont to do, and in a couple years, I graduated with a master's degree in biblical studies from Regent University. During this time, God was fostering an outrageous love for His Word and the One who breathed it into existence in my heart. At last, He showed me what He wanted me to do in this life: teach, write, and help others understand God through His Word. His incredible plan for humanity stretches from the beginning of time until the return of Christ and beyond. This is my first attempt at doing that. I pray God speaks to you as you discover Him who made you, who loves you outrageously, and who works miracles on your behalf.

The opportunity to write and teach this Bible study was born through a strong desire *not* to do a thesis. The last semester of seminary, I had to choose between a practicum and a thesis. So, practicum it was!

My journey toward writing studies began in the spring of 2009, when I took a Bible study class on David, and I fell in love. I fell in love with the God who would choose a shepherd boy who had a sincere love and desire for God. He made some very serious mistakes with very hard consequences, but God made him king over His chosen people, and He would call him a man after God's own heart (Acts 13:22).

I so identified with this man who had such a passionate love for God but somehow kept making the wrong choices. I became hungry to know more about God and how He would accept and rejoice in such a man as David. I was ravenous to know more of Him. I devoured study after study, everything I could get my hands on.

In seminary, God finally began to show me that my hunger for the Word was the cornerstone of the ministry he was developing in my life.

So, when the choice of practicum or thesis was upon me, God placed it in my heart to write and teach a Bible study. My pastor at the time was supportive enough to allow me to teach it at church, and this study of Acts 1–10 was born.

In this study, we are going to journey through the beginnings of the Christian church. As you will hear me harp on over and over and over, this is the story of the early Jewish Christians. These men and women were Jews who believed that Jesus was the Jewish Messiah. They did not yet understand that Jesus was for the world. It is a beautiful look at how God cherished this special time with His covenant people, how He reveled in the salvation of the sons and daughters of Abraham, and how He used them to reach the ends of the earth.

One of the main themes examines how God used miracles to spread His gospel and how He is still using miracles today (you can't study Acts and *not* talk about miracles!). If you learn anything by studying the first ten chapters of Acts with me, I pray you learn that God is *still* a God of miracles. He is working in your life in ways you could never know or suspect. I pray that God blows our faith wide open and that we become men and women of such outrageous faith that we ask huge things of God just to watch Him work! I urge you to keep a prayer journal through this time, and like Paul says in Philippians 4:6–7, "Do not be anxious about anything, but in every situation, through prayer and petition, with thanksgiving, present your requests to God." And more than that—*believe* that He is a good, good Father who answers according to your good.

The second, and most important, theme that this study is working toward is that God is using every situation in these first ten chapters of Acts to open the apostles' minds to sharing the gospel message with every nation and every tongue, every kind of peoples, both Jew and Gentile. God is truly an *impartial* God. He does not conform to social standards, but welcomes every single person into His family. Praise You, Jesus!

This study was written to be utilized in a three-part format. Each week, you will find a commentary and five days of homework—complete with questions. Please begin each week by reading the commentary, which focuses on a very important part of the week's passage. Then proceed to the homework for the day (for each day of the week). Though this study can be used as a personal study, optimally, you will end the week's study with a small group, discussing the questions together as a group.

During the group time, opinions are challenged, understanding is fostered, and faith grows. It will provide you with a safe environment to share your testimony of God's work in your life. It is my sincere hope that you will utilize this study within a group setting and that God will bless your fellowship with increased understanding of His Word, increased faith in His faithfulness and power, and growth of healthy, God-centered relationships.

With so much love and so many blessings,
Audrey

WEEK 1

Commentary: An Introduction to Acts

Welcome, beloved! How excited I am to begin this journey with you. Before we dig into the book of Acts, we need to get the introductory information out of the way so we have a bit of context to help our understanding. So bear with me for today, and then we will get to the good stuff tomorrow!

Unlike some of the books of the Bible, the author of the Acts of the Apostles (Acts) does not name himself. However, we have a very early church father, Irenaeus (ca. AD 130–202), who named the author as Luke in his work *Against Heresies III*. Irenaeus studied under Polycarp, who was a disciple of the apostle John. Therefore, it is assumed that Irenaeus knew that the author's name was Luke, and the name has never been challenged. The author of Acts, henceforth referred to as Luke, is regarded to be a man of substantial learning who is not part of but is in contact with the elite of society. Most believe he was a doctor who was very close with the apostle Paul, and he most likely occasionally traveled with Paul on his missionary journeys.

The Acts of the Apostles was most likely written during the first century (ca. AD 80), and it is written as historiography, which is a factual accounting of chronological events with a focused purpose. It is not scientific in accounting or verbatim; the speeches are condensed into summaries because of their lengths. Because it is written in this manner, Luke salts the historical accounts with his own points of view. We get to see his views on gender roles, theology, Christology, and the purpose of Christianity. I really want you to understand that Luke is *deeply convinced*

1

that Christianity is inclusive to all ethnicities, all social strata, and both genders. We will examine this in much more detail as we move through the book of Acts, but even as we begin this journey, I want you to know to the depths of your spirit that God excludes *no one.*

Luke wrote the book of Acts as a second volume in a two-part series that was meant to be read together, beginning with the gospel of Luke and followed by the book of Acts. Themes that begin in Luke are further explored in Acts, and themes that begin in Acts are built upon foundations laid in Luke. Each covers a span of about thirty years, and they are both about the same number of words; each fills up a single papyrus. Because this is a two-part series, the purpose Luke states in the gospel of Luke 1:1 is applicable to Acts, and it is there that we will find his intended purposes for writing these historical narratives:

> Inasmuch as many have undertaken to compile a narrative of the things that have been accomplished among us, just as those who from the beginning were eyewitnesses and minister of the word have delivered them to us, it seemed good to me also, having followed all things closely for some time past, to write an orderly account for you, most excellent Theophilus, *that you may have certainty* concerning the things you have been taught. (Luke 1:1–4; emphasis added)

Please write the emphasized words here:

Luke's one reason for writing these volumes is that we might have certainty about the *unarguable conclusion* of the gospel. This phrase speaks to unquestionable fact. It means that there is so much evidence that one cannot argue with Luke's conclusion. This means that we can have *certainty* in the unarguable fact of the gospel message—of the events that occur in the life, death, and resurrection of Christ, as well as the events and miracles done by the Holy Spirit through the apostles.

We can rest with certainty in the truth of the life and resurrection of Jesus, and we can have security against the lies of the enemy. Satan twists the truth, and the lies of the world tell us that the gospel message can't possibly be true. The purpose of these books is to give us *security* against all the lies that try to steal the blessings of the truth of salvation in Christ.

Luke addresses a person in the first verses of both Luke and Acts; please look up both Luke 1:1 and Acts 1:1, and write this person's name here:

If you found the name, you noticed that both volumes of Luke's works are written specifically to a man named Theophilus. Most likely, this man provided the funding for Luke's travels and research for this historical project. I like to think of Luke as a reporter and Theophilus as his employer. Luke had two purposes: to record and report the events as truthfully as possible and to convey to Theophilus that the gospel message was true and that it crossed all social strata. This was and is a message for all peoples, and it even attracted the social elite—those with whom Theophilus associated.

Before we get into Acts, I want to point out that neither Luke nor Acts is an eyewitness account. They are reports of historical research taken from eyewitness accounts. Luke's main objective was to record events as accurately as possible, but we see evidence of his own theology and Christology within his narratives. For instance, the examples he gives regarding conversion almost always involved the rich and the poor and both a man and a woman. Luke is exceptionally good at conveying the idea that gender is of no matter to Christ. He is also certain to include many examples of rich and poor men and women converting to the gospel so Theophilus understands that this is not a "poor man's" religion. It is a religion for all humankind.

Tomorrow, you begin your study through Acts—and I cannot even handle the excitement! I hope you are ready for an incredible journey! We are going to learn about God, about His church, and hopefully even a little bit about ourselves. My prayer is that God fills you with a supernatural love for Himself and a supernatural desire for His Word and His presence—that you *hunger* for Him daily. I pray that you fall in love all over again with the miraculous God you serve, and I pray that your faith in Him expands exponentially. Above all, remember that the God who performed incredible miracles during the time of the apostles is the same incredible, miraculous God today.

Week 1: Day 1

Now, we finally get to dig into Acts. I can hardly bear the excitement! Please begin every single day with prayer for an open heart and an open mind, such that God may fill it with His truth, and then turn with me in your Bibles and read Acts 1:1–11.

What we find in this section is the proper rhetoric of the time for introducing a second volume in a series; its purpose is to provide context for the early church beginnings. It reminds the hearer of the message of the first volume in the series—the birth, life, death, and resurrection of Jesus—which sets the stage for the early church as the historiography continues in the second volume.

Each week, we will see and discuss a new miracle in each chapter of Acts. What I love about Acts is that these miracles do not stay on the pages of history; each miracle is something that God is doing in and through our lives and the lives of people around us every single day. My hope and my prayer is that your faith will be strengthened and you will see the power of God in a new and incredible way—one that comes to life and that is not just located in history. I hope that you will see how God's power is still empowering the people of God today to do miraculous things through Jesus Christ. Therefore, as we look at the introduction of Acts 1, Luke is showing us the miracle of Jesus Christ.

I think we begin to take for granted the story of Christ. I know I do, anyway. My prayer for us today is that it hits us anew—and that it grips us to the depths of our being to know that we have a God who planned *from the beginning of time* that He would send His Son to save us. All the way from Genesis 12:3, God reveals His plan for the world. He calls Abram to leave his home and his family and says,

> I will make of you a great nation, and I will bless you and
> make your name great, so that that you will be a blessing.
> I will bless those who bless you, and him who dishonors
> you I will curse, and by you all the families of the earth
> shall be blessed.

God restates this promise to King David in 2 Samuel 7:12–13:

> When your days are fulfilled and you lie down with your
> fathers, I will raise up your offspring after you, who shall
> come from your body, and I will establish his kingdom.
> He shall build a house for my name, and I will establish
> the throne of his kingdom forever.

This passage out of 2 Samuel is what Bible scholars called a double fulfillment prophecy. God very well may begin by speaking literally of Solomon—who does indeed build God's physical temple—but through the sons of Solomon, son of David, Jesus is born. And it is He, Jesus, Son of David, who reigns on the throne for eternity.

As I began researching evidence that God's plan always included Jesus and salvation of the whole earth, I found many incredible prophecies. Some say there are as many as 337 Old Testament prophecies that look forward to the Messiah, but I was not about to verify all of them. However, I did find this awesome chart and was able to verify that the listed prophecies do exactly that. Please pull out your chart and look at appendix 1.

How does it make you feel that Jesus was foreshadowed from the beginning of Jewish history?

What does it tell you about God?

As I was awestruck at God's foreshadowing and foretelling of the coming of His Son, it hit me that every event from the beginning of history was molded by God to bring forth the person and life of Jesus. Really, the person of Jesus and His place in history is, in itself, a miracle.

The idea that He would come from heaven, leave His throne, and live amongst us only to die a horrible death astounds me.

Please summarize or list the prophecies listed in numbers 20-25, 27–34, and 41 on the chart:

None of these things were surprises to Him! He knew of the horrible tragedies that would befall Him, and He still came. Why on earth would He come, knowing all these things He would have to endure? He came to be a sacrifice for our sin. Please fill in the blanks found in Isaiah 53:4–6 (ESV):

> *Surely he has borne our _____*
> *and carried our _____;*
> *yet we esteemed him stricken,*
> *smitten by God, and afflicted.*
> *But he was pierced for our _____;*
> *he was crushed for our _____;*
> *upon him was the chastisement that brought us _____,*
> *and with his wounds we are _____.*
> *All we like sheep have gone astray;*
> *we have turned—every one—to his own way;*
> *and the LORD has laid on him*
> *the iniquity of us all.*

Even though He knew He would be persecuted, betrayed, tortured, and murdered, Jesus came because He loves you more than you can ever comprehend. Now, go back through the scripture listed above and mark out every "our" or "we" you can find and replace it with "me," "my" or "I."

There is no greater miracle than the love of Christ. He is the miracle that brings every good thing into our lives; He is the miracle that breaks our chains and sets us free from any guilt or shame. Through the miracle of Christ, our days are full of peace and joy, and our futures are full of hope and excitement. As we begin our journey through Acts, we look first to Christ; without Him, without His sacrifice, there is nothing worth studying. "Every good and perfect gift comes from the God of lights, of whom there is no shadow or variation due to change" (James 1:17). Jesus is the most perfect gift we could ever receive. If you have not yet received Him as your Savior, please speak to a trusted Christian friend, pastor, or family member about how to become a follower of Christ.

Jesus, I praise your most holy name. Your love is unparalleled, and Your grace is unfathomable. You look at each one of us and see the child You created; You call to us unceasingly. How I praise You that You do not give up on any single one! I pray for Your beloved—who has chosen to take this journey through the beginning of Acts—that You would light their hearts on *fire* for You! I pray that You would speak Your message into them and reveal Yourself to them through this study. I pray that You would give them a supernatural faith and love and desire to know You more. I pray Your blessings upon them as they strive to serve You with their time and actions, God. It is in Your most precious and holy name. Amen.

Week 1: Day 2

I am so glad you are doing your reading this week. I promise it will be interesting because God's Word always is. I hope you will even learn a bit. Before you get started, please pray that God will open your ears to hear the message He wants to share with you. Pray that He will speak a fresh message into your heart today.

As you read, please remember to record any verse that God speaks specifically to you today and any words He gives you that you might be willing to share at our next discussion. Please read Acts 1:6–11.

Before Jesus ascends into heaven, He orders the disciples to gather together in Jerusalem and await the baptism of the Holy Spirit. They did not understand Jesus's words and were instead awaiting His transformation into the promised Messiah that they understood. After Babylonian exile, Jews began to believe that the Messiah would be the one to rid their society of "alien impositions, usually by military means."[1] The apostles wanted to see Jesus, the Warrior King—not Jesus the Sacrificial Lamb. They simply did not understand God's plan.

How often do we assume God's plan and His motives only to find out we had no idea what He had in mind? I know I do! I try to put God's plan into my own context and usually underestimate the plan. We cannot conceive of the goals of God because they far surpass our wildest dreams. God will always do *immeasurably more* than we could ever imagine (Ephesians 3:20).

Please use the space below to reflect on a time in your life when you assumed you knew God's plan and He did so much more than you had planned:

---

[1] Harris Lenowitz, *The Jewish Messiahs: From the Galilee to Crown Heights* (New York: Oxford University Press, 1998) 23.

God did not want to save just the Jews. He wanted to save *the whole world*. In His reply, Jesus tried to give them a clearer idea of what their futures held: empowerment through the Holy Spirit, witnessing throughout the entire world.

What do you think was going through the apostles' minds as they heard Jesus's directions for the future?

After Jesus ascends into heaven, the disciples are standing there and looking for Him when two angels appear and state the obvious: Jesus has been taken to His home in heaven. I just love that. Sometimes, we are so busy waiting to see God in something that we miss what He is just saying, "It is what it is. Now get a move on." In this event, He knew it would take something fierce for the disciples to get the hint, so He sent some angels to tell the apostles for Him.

Has there ever been a time in your life when you were waiting for God to show up—in a relationship, in an undertaking, or in a goal—when He was just waiting on you to move onto something bigger and better?

If there is something in your life right now that you think God is telling you that it's time to simply move on, write a prayer to Him right here and ask for His direction.

Nothing feels better than giving God the weight that has been pressing upon you. Revel and rejoice in your freedom!

Week 1: Day 3

Good day to you, dearest one! I pray that God has begun to fill you with excitement for His Word and a desire to learn more about Him. Please turn to God in prayer, asking Him to fill you with excitement for His Word and to give you a fresh understanding and a new insight into His book of Acts as you study with Him today. And then please read Acts 1:12–20.

After the disciples return to Jerusalem, they return to the upper room where they were staying. While the host is not named in this instance, I want to point out that, throughout the book of Acts, Luke takes a major interest in the lodgings of Christians.[2] There are quite a few times that Luke mentions people's names solely because they hosted Peter or Paul or other Christian missionaries (9:42, 17:5–9, 21:8–9, 21:16, 28:7). There are two times that Luke actually gives the complete address of where Peter or Paul were staying: in 9:11 with Judas on Strait Street in Damascus and in 10:5–6 at Simon the tanner's in the house by the sea in Joppa. While this may seem very random and insignificant, it is very important to Luke to recognize these people.

Why do you think Luke made a point of specifically naming these gracious hosts?

Luke's second volume is about the spread of the Word and those who made it possible. Thus, these people (and their places of lodging) who are not significant actors in the story itself, are referred to as *vital supporters* to the movement.

There is such a beautiful lesson to be learned here. Luke goes to

---

[2] Ben Witherington III, *The Acts of the Apostles: A Socio-rhetorical Commentary* (Grand Rapids, MI: W.B. Eerdmans Pub., 1998) 166.

great effort to tell of those who simply supplied an overnight stay for the Christian teachers—he names them as *vital* to the mission of Christ. How many of us see our positions in the body of Christ as miniscule or unimportant? So many of us have heard that every position is vital, but we have a hard time accepting it. From the very beginning of Acts, Luke shows us that the smallest things, like simple hospitality, are *invaluable* in the kingdom of God. God takes a small boy's lunch to feed five thousand men—and probably more than fifteen thousand people. Never doubt that *your gift*, no matter how small, is utterly vital to the kingdom of heaven.

Please write a prayer praising God for your gift and the work He does through you and the joy He brings to you because of it. If you feel like your gift, and maybe even you as a person, is unimportant to the kingdom of heaven, write a prayer asking God to show you how to use your gift, how He accomplishes great things through you, and how He brings you indescribable joy in using it for His glory.

So, let's get back to the scene that is being described in the upper room. This is such an interesting scene to me. What on earth are these men doing? What does it matter if there are eleven or twelve disciples? Really. Who cares? Clearly they did.

Why do you think it was important to them to fill the place vacated by Judas the betrayer?

First and foremost, we need to understand that these men were *Jewish men for the Jewish people*. In the first couple of chapters of Acts, the apostles' primary concern was for the Jews in Jerusalem. The Gentiles are not even a thought in their heads at this point. We cannot look at these men simply as the first Christians. They are Jews, thinking they are there to spread a message to the Jews about how God has finally saved *the Jews*. They did *not* understand the total implications of salvation in relation to the Law; they did *not* think of their message as "Christianity." They were simply prophets in a long line of prophets throughout Jewish history, coming to share God's latest message to *the Jews*.

Accordingly, we find Luke implicating a number of Jewish customs that would have been evident to first-century Jewish readers. One of the first things Peter says is that the "Scripture had to be fulfilled" (Acts 1:16). Peter points out that God's plan was set in motion long before the events occurred, and the prophecies must be fulfilled. Therefore, we see Peter quoting David in Psalms 69:25 and 108:7–8: "When [a wicked man] is tried, let him come forth guilty; let his prayer be counted as sin! May his days be few; may another take his office!" When a guilty man's office is vacated, it needs to be filled again in order to restore that office.

We actually learn a little about the office in question by the number found in verse 15: Luke tells that 120 people were present when Peter stands up to approach the issue of replacing Judas. This is significant because, in Jewish tradition, 120 is the smallest population that could have its own council. Tradition states that each councilman (or judge) should represent at least ten members.[3] Therefore, having 120 members promotes the idea that twelve councilmen (witnesses) are needed in order to complete the council. Apart from that line of thought, almost certainly one reason for adding a twelfth witness is because of the tradition of the twelve tribes of Israel. Luke is concerned about restoring to *full strength* the group whose "primary role" is regarded to be their relationship with Israel.[4]

Never forget that God is completely concerned that His church is at full strength. What that means for us is that each one of us is:

- We must be participating in a faithful relationship with Christ. To be faithful to Christ means that we spend time with Him daily. We are told by Paul in 1 Thessalonians 5:17 to pray without

---

[3] William H. Willimon, "Acts," In *Interpretation Bible Commentary* (Louisville, KY: John Knox Press, 1988) 23.

[4] Witherington, *The Acts of the Apostles: A Socio-Rhetorical Commentary*, 116.

ceasing; God is supposed to be our best friend! You know you talk to and text your bestie all the time—God is meant to be so much more in our lives than any person ever could be—so treat Him accordingly. He desires time and a relationship with us; give Him that time, and you will find your life entirely changed for the better. Further more, how do we know God's voice as He speaks to us unless we acquaint ourselves with His words? Get to know Him through His Word breathed onto the page of the holy scriptures. That is how we will know His voice of truth as He whispers His love, direction, conviction, and encouragements into our hearts.

- We must be bearing a *fruit* in our walk with Christ. Jesus says that we will know if people are false or true by the fruit they bear (Matthew 7:16). James 2:14–17 tells us that faith without works is a dead faith. One is not more important than the other; rather, one thrives in tandem with the other. If we have a faithful walk with Christ, we cannot help but bear fruit through the outpouring of His spirit (Galatians 5:22-23).

- We must be using our God-given gifts to bring Him glory. God breathed life into you, and with that breath came gifts unique to you so that you are equipped for every good work God has planned in advance for you to do (Ephesians 2:10). God will allow you to use them however you choose, but if you use them to bring God glory, you will find yourself filled with a sense of purpose, fulfillment, and utter joy that you will never find anywhere else. God breathed life into you as He planned every one of your days; your life will shine the brightest when walking within His plan.

You are God's church, and you are the tabernacle where God makes His home. He wants you at full strength because He knows that with His power, you can do *incredible things* for the kingdom of heaven. I pray that God reveals every single one of your gifts to you and makes it abundantly clear where He wants you to use them in each day so that you may be blessed and He may be glorified.

Week 1: Day 4

Yesterday, we left off with the *why* of replacing Judas. Today, we want to look at the *how*. As always, please pray for understanding and knowledge as we read God's Word today. Then read Acts 1:21–26.

What were the requirements to qualify as a replacement disciple?

What men fulfilled the aforementioned requirements?

How did the apostles choose the man to replace Judas?

In verses 21–22, Peter comes up with a plan to replace him with one of the men who have accompanied them during "all the time that the Lord Jesus went in and out among us, beginning from the baptism of John until the day when he was taken up from us—one of these men must become with us a witness to his resurrection." They determined that Barsabbas and Matthias fit these aforementioned criteria, and they *prayed*. So many times, the apostles just didn't quite get it as they walked with Jesus, but this time, they did. They prayed, knowing that God was the *only* one who could see into the hearts of the impending replacements (1 Samuel 16:7) and wisely called upon the Lord to decide.

Is there something in your life that needs to be prayed over, but you simply haven't prayed about it yet?

Sometimes, we choose not to pray because we fear of God's answer. Sometimes, we just do not think that God cares. Whatever is stopping you from taking "that thing" to the Lord—remember, He already knows it intimately anyway. He is just waiting on you to take it to Him so He can show you that He does, in fact, care very much about anything and everything that is going on in your life. If there is something going on in your life right now that is causing you any stress, anxiety, or heartache, give it to Him right now—and keep giving it over to Him every day until He answers you. I implore you to write it in your prayer journal and trust that God is going to answer in the exact way you would want if you knew all the things He did about your life.

After the disciples prayed, they cast lots. The casting of lots was an ancient custom allowed by God for the Hebrews to determine His will in certain situations. In the Old Testament, humanity did not have the indwelling of the Holy Spirit, which is what guides us in God's will. Therefore, the casting of lots was one way that God would reveal His will to them. This was not a common practice in Jewish tradition, but it was sanctioned by God in specific circumstances.[5]

Please read these next few verses and summarize what happened in each one:

Leviticus 16:8

Numbers 26:55

---

[5] Anne Marie Kitz, "The Hebrew Terminology of Lot Casting and Its Ancient Near Eastern Context," *Catholic Biblical Quarterly* 62, no. 2 (April 2000): 209. Accessed May 20, 2015. ATLA Religion Database [EBSCO].

1 Chronicles 25:8

Matthew 27:35

As you can see, casting of lots was a common practice. In the Old Testament, these were ways that the Hebrews asked for God's guidance and trusted Him to turn the lots the way He desired.

What was the one outlier in the bunch?

I listed the scene out of Matthew to show you that people often used casting of lots in unrighteous ways. Everything God gives us can be twisted into something sinful. Every characteristic we have in our spirits comes from our Creator—from our love and compassion to our anger, jealousy, and pride. Each trait God placed within us mirrors a trait within Him; in our humanity, we allow it to turn into something sinful instead of using it to promote holiness and righteousness. Jesus allowed Himself to be nailed to the cross so that you could be restored and redeemed into holiness and righteousness. Do not despise any characteristic God has given you; it was placed there with precision and purpose. Instead, ask God to show you how to tame it with self-control and how to use it for His glory.

As we move back to Acts 1, we have to remember that the apostles did not yet have the indwelling of the Holy Spirit and the guidance it brings. God allowed them to use the casting of lots to determine His will in choosing the twelfth disciple. God chose Matthias, and he is henceforth counted as one of the twelve apostles.

Week 1: Day 5

Today is our last day of homework this first week of study. Congratulations! You made it through! I thank you for taking the time to learn about this first chapter of Acts and the foundational information that sets the stage for the rest of our study. Now that we have made our way through the entirety of the first chapter of Acts, I want to take a look at the overarching theme of the whole chapter. Please reread Jesus's command to the apostles found in Acts 1:4–5.

What were they told to do?

In short, they were told to wait. Is there anything more discouraging than waiting on God sometimes? I am a woman of action, and there is nothing harder for me than hearing the word *wait* from my heavenly Father. I won't go into the importance of waiting on God's time today because we are going to look into that at a later time; however, I do want to look at what you do *while* you are waiting. If you don't remember from this week, scan back over verses 12–26 to remind yourself what the apostles did while waiting.

Please summarize it here:

Just because God asks us to wait doesn't mean that we are idle. The past year has been exceedingly hard for me. I taught a Bible study that was extremely successful, and I was fired up and ready to dive into Bible study ministry. It was precisely in that moment that all doors shut in my face. I was also serving as a volunteer in youth ministry, but I knew that youth ministry would not be my career. I was serving, enjoying it, and loving the incredible students I served, but I was also discontent.

I felt like I was not doing what God had created me to do, and I did not know why He had closed all the doors to continue teaching Bible study. Over the past couple months, however, God started showing me that the love I was pouring on those students was exactly what I should have been doing during that time.

Just because I was waiting on God to open doors into Bible study ministry doesn't mean that serving in youth ministry was anything less than of the utmost importance. The waiting didn't make the opportunities for serving any less important to His kingdom. He was giving me opportunities to serve Him well, and He was preparing me for the path He had laid before me. I have said it before, and I will say it again: beloved, your God is *good*, especially in the waiting.

I praise Him for giving me a period of waiting because of all the work He did in me during that time. I also praise Him because of the work He allowed me to do for His kingdom during this time. I realized that I have a sincere love for high school students, and God gave me an opportunity to love and enjoy them, share my experiences, share my testimony, and share the goodness of God. This time of waiting was a blessing for me.

Please share a time when God asked you to serve in His kingdom in a way that surprised you and your resulting experience:

The disciples were not idle while they were waiting. They used the time to prepare for their future ministry. They used the time to fulfill the twelve-seated office of the apostleship. Not only did they need to fill the office left vacant by Judas the Betrayer, but the number twelve held extreme importance to a culture based heavily on symbolism.

Can you think of any significant symbolism the number twelve holds for the Jews?

If you are familiar with the Old Testament, you may remember that Jacob, later renamed "Israel" by God, was the father of the twelve tribes of the Israelites. Twelve is a number of completion and perfection in the Bible; therefore, the twelve tribes indicated completeness within the Israelite nation.

With the symbolism behind the number twelve, it is easy to understand why Jesus wanted twelve disciples. It is the number of completion, and it symbolizes a new era in God's kingdom. Jacob was the father of the twelve tribes of Israel, who were meant to be God's light to the world.[6] Jesus had come to be the father of the new era of God's kingdom. Therefore, he chose twelve who would symbolize the perfection and completeness of this new covenant[7] that he came to provide for the entire world. The disciples obviously wanted to continue the symbolism of twelve apostles; they cast lots to learn of God's will in picking their twelfth member.

I love that God always has something for us to do for Him. He may give us a main objective for the future, but while He is working all things out so the future is successful, He fills our "waiting" with meaningful acts of service and ministry. He constantly provides opportunities for us to be a part of His magnificent plan for this world. What a gracious God we serve, that He would allow us to take part in His kingdom. Amen!

At the end of every week, I am going to ask you some questions. They are really general questions that will allow you to share what God is doing in and through you throughout the course of our time together in Acts. My prayer is that it will provide opportunities for you to share your testimony of God's work in your life with your small group and increase your faith in God.

---

[6] Genesis 12:2–3

[7] Hebrews 9:15

What have you learned during your reading time?

Did God speak a specific verse or concept to you over the course of your readings? Please take a minute to write down what God revealed to you:

It is my sincere belief and prayer that God is going to move mountains in our lives in this study. What mountain do you need moved in your life? What thing do you want to give over to God? Will you write it here and promise to trust Him with your burden? Will you let Him take it over and trust Him to work a miracle for you? If you will, write your prayer and your promise here:

Dearest Lord, You are the revealer of all things. Thank You for constantly teaching us new things, for speaking new words, and for putting ideas into our hearts and minds. I pray You bless us for our diligence and change our hearts to be more like You through the study of Your Word. Lord, I know You are the Miracle Worker. I know You are Sovereign. I pray that You take over and blow our minds through this study. I pray that You work miracles in our lives, break strongholds, free us from bondage, redeem us, and heal us in our brokenness. Increase our faith, Lord, and show Your Mighty Hand! I thank You for Your son, Jesus Christ, for Your sacrifice, for Your inexplicable love and mercy. I bless Your name, O God. I praise You, for You are *worthy*! In Your most holy and precious name. Amen.

Thank you for taking the time to join me in your readings this week. I pray you are finding the first chapter of Acts as fascinating as I do and that you might have even learned a little bit. I know that God is going to do incredible things in and through us as we study together. Amen.

WEEK 2
Commentary: The Miracle of the Holy Spirit

Today, we approach the infamous Acts 2. This chapter of scripture is the basis of many theological issues that divide the church today. At the same time, it provides a perfect example of what a church in Christ should look like. Underscoring both of these themes, however, is the power of the Holy Spirit. Accordingly, our miracle for the week is the Holy Spirit. Before we get into the text, however, I want to give you some background.

The word for *Holy Spirit* in the Old Testament Hebrew is *ruach*; in New Testament Greek, it is *pneuma*. Both words mean wind, breath, and spirit. The idea of the Holy Spirit is something that has been around since the beginning of Genesis. Genesis 1:2 says that Spirit of God hovered over the face of the waters; in Genesis 1:26, God says, "Let *us* make man in *our* image."

Interestingly enough, the Hebrew word for *God is 'elohiym*; the very word itself is plural. For all intents and purposes, it means "gods." Both we and the Hebrews understand the word to describe our One and Only God, YHWH, Creator, Father, but the word itself is plural. I cannot believe that was accidental. From the very first chapter of the Bible, God gives us clues to His nature—He is three in one. He is the Father, Son, and Holy Spirit. He is three, yet He is very much one. I just love how God reveals Himself to us over and over and over, don't you? The part of God that draws our focus today is the Holy Spirit.

In the Old Testament, the Holy Spirit was listed as the source, the giver of life. Job 33:4 says, "The Spirit has made me, the breath of the Almighty gives me life." God the Father created our bodies, but the Holy Spirit breathes life into us. There are multiple instances in the OT of the Spirit descending on a specific person for a specific time or task—the builders of the Ark of the Covenant,[8] the heroic judges like Deborah, Gideon, and Samson,[9] and King Saul.[10] However, there is only one time recorded in ancient history before the realization of Christ that the Holy Spirit descended upon a person and did not leave: King David. First Samuel 16: 13 says, "Then Samuel took the horn of oil and anointed [David] in the midst of his brothers. And the Spirit of the Lord rushed upon David from that day forward." What this means is that God is blessedly *sovereign*. As a rule, the Holy Spirit would not reside indefinitely within a person until that person had been reconciled through the sacrifice and glorification of Christ. However, when God has a purpose and wants to do something for the glory of His kingdom, you better believe He can do whatever He wants! What the examples of the Holy Spirit in the OT do attest, however, is that the Holy Spirit was *present* and *active* in the Bible long before the New Testament.

In the New Testament, however, the Holy Spirit takes a much more prominent role. John 7:39 tells us that the Holy Spirit could not be given until Jesus was glorified. So, in Acts 1:4 Jesus told the disciples to await the promise of the Father. This promise came from the prophet Ezekiel when he prophesied about the Spirit in Ezekiel 37:27: "My dwelling place will be with them; I will be their God, and they will be my people." Romans 8:11 says, "But if the Spirit of Him who raised Jesus from the dead dwells in you, He who raised Christ Jesus from the dead will also give life to your mortal bodies through His Spirit who dwells in you." We call this the "indwelling of the Holy Spirit." The indwelling of the Spirit occurs at the very moment that you put your faith in God and accept Jesus as Lord over your life. At that moment, the Spirit rushes upon you and makes its dwelling place—its tabernacle within you—forever.

It is the Holy Spirit who gives us life and takes the spiritually dead and raises them up to eternal life with Christ. The Spirit raises us up as

---

[8] Exodus 35:30–35
[9] Judges 4:4–5; 6:34; 14:6
[10] 1 Samuel 11:6

a new creation, and He transforms us according to 2 Corinthians 3:18. In Galatians 5:22–23, Paul says that people will know we are Christians because of the fruit we bear in the Spirit: love, joy, peace, patience, kindness, goodness, faithfulness, gentleness, and self-control. I have given you a list of all the names and purposes of the Holy Spirit as He lives within us in appendix 2.

- He is the one who whispers the invitation of relationship with God into our hearts.

- He is the one who gives us desire for more than the empty life of the world.

- He lives within us because, once He's invited, He can't bear to leave our sides.

- He is the one who renews us, gives us peace, guides us, helps us, and transforms us.

- He is the Revealer, our link to God. It is the voice through which God speaks His instruction, His love, His pleasure, and His joy in us—and His disappointment and condemnation of our actions. It is the source of all hope, all joy, all love, all direction in our lives, and all healing of our broken hearts. It is the power by which we are transformed into the likeness of Christ and by whom we have access to power beyond our wildest imaginations. Through faith in the Holy Spirit, we can literally move mountains, heal the sick and broken, cast out demons, and perform any manner of miracles. The gift of the Holy Spirit is not something tame and weak; it is wild and powerful, and it empowers us in ways that we do not even realize.

It is the empowerment of the Holy Spirit that brings us to Acts 2:1–4 (ESV):

> [1] When the day of Pentecost arrived, they were all together in one place. [2] And suddenly there came from heaven a sound like a mighty rushing wind, and it filled the entire house where they were sitting. [3] And divided tongues as of fire appeared to them and rested on each one of them. [4] And they were all filled with the Holy Spirit and began to speak in other tongues as the Spirit gave them utterance.

As verse 1 says, this is the scene of Pentecost. The disciples have been waiting in the upper room, and the promise of God is finally fulfilled. The Holy Spirit rushes upon them, and they immediately began to speak in tongues. Throughout Acts, speaking in tongues is Luke's way of describing the *manifestation of the Spirit* in and through us.

For Luke, the baptism of the Spirit was not just an empowerment of the Spirit for empowerment's sake—nothing with God is ever for show. Rather, the baptism of the Spirit in Acts was, and still is to this day, an *activating empowerment* so that the believer is empowered to be a witness for God. In Acts, this was shown by speaking tongues because the main purpose of the early church was to spread the message unto the ends of the earth.[11]

For the church's modern purposes, charismatics believe specifically that being baptized in the Spirit is a sign that you have been called to the ministry of spreading the Word of God, not unlike the first-century apostles. That is not to say in any form or fashion that tongues is the only gift that signifies the baptism of the Spirit. Instead, God equips us with the gift needed to fulfill His calling over our lives—be it tongues to speak in languages other than our own, the gift of speech to allow His words to pour from our lips, the gift of encouragement to uplift another, or the gift of endurance to run His race through the end. Whatever the gift may be, it is solely to the glory of He who gives in abundance.

The baptizing of the Spirit also had a specific purpose for the direction of first-century apostles. It proved without a doubt that a person had put his or her faith in God. This becomes especially important when the

---

[11] Acts 1:8

disciples are forced out of Jerusalem and begin to spread the gospel to the Gentiles. Last week, we discussed that these men were Jewish and believed that they were simply Jewish prophets empowered to tell their fellow Jews about the next thing God had done and was doing in the Jewish community. We will discuss this more later, but I want you to understand the purpose of Luke's pneumatology (Holy Spirit beliefs). Being baptized in the Spirit was a sign that God allowed and desired even the Gentiles to be in his family as well. Since Luke's main purpose of writing Acts was to provide evidence that the gospel of Jesus Christ was for all peoples, nations, and tongues, the baptism of the Spirit was an outward sign that God had accepted the Gentile peoples in a way in which no Jew could argue.

The baptism of the Spirit acted as a guide of sorts to lead the apostles to witness to the Gentiles, and the miracles they did through the Spirit gave credence to their gospel message of Jesus Christ. The Jews believed that miracles could only be done in God, so the miracles the apostles performed, including the speaking of tongues in Acts 2, made it harder to discredit their message.

Here's what I want you to understand today: the power given to the first-century apostles through the Holy Spirit is still available to you today! We have been trained by the church to believe in the salvation of Christ, the forgiveness of sins, and the renewing of our spirits, but the church often forgets to teach us that we have access to the incredible power of the Holy Spirit.

In chapter 1 of *Forgotten God*, Francis Chan says, "If you or I had never been to a church and had read only the Old and New Testaments, we would have *significant expectations* of the Holy Spirit in our lives … but we don't live this way. For some reason, we don't think we need the Holy Spirit. We don't expect the Holy Spirit to act." When was the last time you had *high* expectations for the Holy Spirit? Do you remember a time when you asked something miraculous of God and truly believed that He would do it?

In my life, I have all the head knowledge and belief in the world that God can do *whatever* he chooses to do. However, I simply did not think He would do it for *me*. Can you relate to that? We, the people of God, the tabernacle of His Spirit, need to renew our faith in His power. We need to believe to the depths of our beings that we are filled with the untapped power of God. Jesus tells the disciples in Matthew 10:8 to go proclaiming the kingdom of God, to heal the sick, cast out demons, cleanse the lepers, and raise the dead.

When we are focused on the kingdom of God, when our sole purpose is to give Him glory and add numbers to the kingdom, God will empower us to do miracles we could never imagine without Him. Jesus says if we have the faith of a mustard seed, we can move mountains. Do you truly believe that? Do you believe that God will come through for you—not in your head, not just that He is able—and that He loves you enough to show up in your moment of need?

The first few verses of Acts 2 are but the tip of the iceberg; as you read Acts, I want you to list the miracles God does through His people. As you are doing that, please remember to write your prayers in your own prayer journal and mark and date when God answers them. He is still at work through His people today; what would happen if we had the faith of the mustard seed? I fully believe that we will see a revival of epic proportions if we unleash the power of the Spirit in this world. Let's pray that God will give us the faith to move mountains and the desire to bring glory to Him in incredible ways through the power of His Spirit.

Week 2: Day 1

I am so excited to take the journey of Acts 2 with you! This is a fairly long chapter, so I pray that you will have endurance and persevere through the last day. I know that God will bless your efforts in spending time with Him and His Word. Just as we did last week, please be aware and record the verse or idea that God gives you that you may be willing to share in our discussion next week. Before we start, please take a few moments to pray that God reveals something new to you today and that He speaks a fresh word into your heart. Please open your Bibles to Acts 2 and read verses 1–4.

Last week, Jesus asked the disciples to stay together in Jerusalem and await the promise of the Father (Acts 1:4). As we see in 2:1, the disciples did as Jesus asked and stayed together until the promise of the Father was realized. After the persecution of Jesus, they had to think they were in danger of the same fate. They had to have been scared for their lives, yet they stayed. I wonder if through the fear, there was a curiosity and maybe excitement for the promise to be fulfilled. In John 16:7, Jesus says to the disciples, "Nevertheless, I tell you the truth: it is to your advantage that I go away, for if I do not go away, the Helper will not come to you. But if I go, I will send him to you."

Why do you think it was to their *advantage* that Jesus leaves so the Helper could come?

What advantages are there in having the Helper, the Spirit of God, dwell within you?

God gives far more abundantly than we expect. It may not be when we want it or how we want it to happen, but in His perfect time, He gives in abundance. We just have to hold on until the blessing comes.

I love the imagery in Acts 2:2: the sound of the mighty rushing wind that fills the entire house. It's no coincidence that Luke describes the sound as a great rushing wind because it was, in fact, just that. If you remember from the week two commentary, the word *spirit* means wind or breath. Can you just imagine God breathing down on the disciples and filling them with His Spirit? Take a moment to close your eyes and picture this scene.

What do you see? What do you hear? What do you smell?

I think of Moses as he comes down from speaking with God and the need for him to cover his face because he glowed from coming in contact with God's Shekinah (God's glory) (Exodus 34). I wonder if the disciples glowed in the moment that God's Spirit came upon them and shone with His power and glory for just an instant. I imagine them erupting in shouts and songs of praise as they are filled with unspeakable joy—each in a different language as the gift of tongues came upon them. What a beautiful scene!

They were the first in the New Testament period to receive this gift, but—praise God—they are not the last! The incredible and humbling thing about God is that the minute we speak Jesus as our Savior and ask for His forgiveness, the *pneuma*, the Holy Spirit, rushes upon on us as we are born again. Again, it is no accident that *ruach* and *pneuma* mean "breath." God breathed His spirit into Adam to give him mortal life and each life after him, but God also breathes new life into each Christian the moment he or she accepts Christ.

I find it beautifully balanced that each time we begin new life, God is the one who breathes it into us. At our first conception, God breathes and fills our barely-there bodies with our spirits; at our choice of a new life, borne of the blood Christ spilled on the cross, God breathes into us again and we are renewed and filled with *His Spirit*. What beautiful symmetry!

From the very second we choose to live a life in Jesus, God breathes His Spirit into us and we are immediately filled. Many of us do not always feel it in that moment, but the Spirit is there, just waiting for you to open yourself to its presence. Even more, there is nothing you can ever do in this life that will cause Him to leave you. "For I will never leave nor forsake you," says the LORD.[12]

Describe what it means to know that God will live in you forever and will never leave or forsake you:

In your darkest hour, in your moment of need, in your time of depression or desolation, He is there. Such an incredible thought, isn't it? Praise His holy and precious name! Amen.

---

[12] Deuteronomy 31:6, ESV

Week 2: Day 2

Good day to you! I thank God that you are being faithful to the study of His Word and pray that you are enjoying every bit of it! I am praying that God is truly speaking to you and growing your love for Him and His Word every single day. I am praying that He blesses you for your efforts. Now, as always, please take a moment for yourself and pray that God speaks to you through this next section of Acts. Please take a moment to now read Acts 2:5–13.

Jerusalem was a melting pot of peoples; it was a place in which all had to travel through to get from Asia or Rome to Egypt and vice versa. It was also where the temple of God was built, so it drew Jews from every nation. The events we read about in chapter 2 of Acts are known to us as the Pentecost, the time that the Holy Spirit first fell upon believers. What is so interesting is that the time of Pentecost occurred during the Festival of Weeks (the Jewish celebration of God's faithfulness to His covenant made with Abraham), which drew in Jewish peoples to Jerusalem to celebrate the festival. I love the symbolism in the timing. God fulfilled His promise to Abraham to bless every nation and tongue through his ancestry during the very festival that celebrates God's faithfulness to His promises. God is a master of symmetry and imagery!

As we learned in the commentary, the disciples received the gift of tongues so they may teach the Word of God to all peoples from every nation. Throughout Acts, you will notice that Luke uses the manifestation of the gift of tongues—both for translational purposes as well as ecstatic speech praising God—to provide proof that one has indeed been baptized in the Spirit.

Do you believe that the gift of tongues is still given today?

What do you think the purpose might be?

Of what did the disciples speak in verse 11 once they received the gift of tongues?

When we have been blessed with a spiritual gift, it is *only ever* for the purpose of bringing glory to God!

Did you notice the reason for the drawing of the crowd in verse 6? They heard the sound of the Holy Spirit! I wonder if God made the baptism of the Spirit audible during the Pentecost because He was impatient for them to start teaching all the nations. He just made a really big noise and used their natural curiosity to bring them all together before the apostles.

I just love the people's reaction—bewilderment! I can only imagine that we must bewilder those who do not understand Christianity with our actions and beliefs. I pray that we reflect God in our lives so strongly that those who watch us can only be amazed and perplexed and ask, "What does this mean (v. 12)?"

In verse 13, we see the haters. Even back in the day, haters were making fun of those they didn't understand. I would suggest that we all have a bit of the hater in us. Don't we all see what we want to see and dismiss the amazing for something mundane? If we do not have faith that God can and will make miracles on our behalf or on the behalf of others, we will not see the miracles for what they are. Instead, we will write them off as coincidences or something else.

Have you ever seen a miracle happen? If so, what?

In December 2012, my dad died. He was in the hospital for two weeks because of a gallstone that caused pancreatitis. They told us that it was not a matter of *if* he went home but *when*. He was only fifty-two, he was healthy, and it was just a gallstone! After the first week in the hospital, my mom would go home to shower and change clothes once a day. As she continued this routine, she noticed three little green stalks popping out of the frozen ground in front of the house. In December, absolutely nothing should be growing. For the next week, as my dad was still trying to recover but not getting any better, my mom continued to notice these stalks as they grew. My dad passed on December 18, 2012, at 10:01 a.m. When we came home from the hospital, my mom noticed that the stalks had blossomed into three white flowers just that morning—between nine and eleven. In the front of the garden, there was nothing white to drop seeds. Was it a miracle? Absolutely. The flowers did not pop out of nowhere; God knew the exact moment he was bringing my father home and brought the flowers forth to speak a message of love and comfort to my mom in the very moment she needed it most.

Miracles can be small—speaking only to the one who needs a moment of encouragement—or they can be front and center, speaking the message of salvation in Christ in myriad languages. God performs miracles for all different reasons, but they always they speak love, hope, and His glory!

As you go through this day, I pray that God opens your eyes to the works of His hands—every creature great and small speaks His glory. Let Him show off and praise Him for the incredible Creator that He is!

Week 2: Day 3

This day is kind of out of place, but it is one of my favorites. Please bear with me. We are going to look at the context of the Pentecost a little bit deeper today, and we will be reviewing some of the things we have already learned. As always, please spend some time with God in prayer before you begin. Please skim or reread Acts 2:1–14 to remind yourself of the events.

If you remember from yesterday, this event takes place during a huge celebration—one of the biggest festivals of the year for the Jews: the Feast of Weeks. This festival draws all the Jews who are able to travel to Jerusalem: Jews from Parthia, Media, Elam, peoples of Mesopotamia, Judea, Cappadocia, Pontus, Asia, Phrygia, Pamphylia, Egypt, and parts of Libya, Rome, Crete, and Arabia (2:9–11). Beginning in verse 14, Peter calls all the men of Judea and all who are in Jerusalem—he was speaking to hundreds, if not thousands of men from at least fifteen countries—and asks them to hear and know the words he is about to impart.

I know we discussed the significance of the festival in yesterday's lesson, and I don't want to beat a dead horse, but I simply must point out the timing of this event. The Feast of Weeks was fifty days after Passover. Jesus was crucified at nine o'clock in the morning on Passover—the exact time of the first sacrifice in the Jewish temple—and he died six hours later at three o'clock—the exact time of the second sacrifice in the Jewish temple. (I won't go into any detail, but the timing of his death is amazing. According to the Jewish traditions, He was the sacrifice in every way).

He rose from the grave three days later and showed Himself to many people for forty days before He ascended into heaven (Acts 1:2–11). However, in His last appearance to the apostles, Jesus told them that the Holy Spirit would come upon them. He told them to wait in the city until this happens—before they went out into their ministry (Luke 24:49). If the Feast of Weeks was fifty days after Passover, and Jesus died on Passover and rose three days later for the next forty days, there were at least seven days that the apostles had to wait before God sent the Holy Spirit upon them. For seven days, they had no clue what was going to happen—or when.

There comes a time in our lives where we are simply told by God to *wait*. Most of the time, we do not know why, what will happen next, or when it will happen. We are just told to wait. And that is what we have to do if we want to be faithful to God and the plan He has for our lives. This waiting can be some of the most trying times of our lives. For me, it typically comes when I am on fire for God and so excited to do His work, and then He tells me to do nothing.

What happens when you are excited and ready to move on something and all you get is a big, fat *wait*?

If you are anything like me, it can be frustrating, discouraging, or deflating. It is so hard to keep your excitement for ministry when you have no idea what you are supposed to do next and God just keeps telling you to wait. Can you imagine the disciples' excitement and the fire in their hearts when they saw Jesus raised from the dead? They knew their Messiah had come, and they wanted nothing more than to tell their fellow Jews—and then Jesus told them to wait.

Why did Jesus want them to wait?

We hear all the time that God's timing is perfect. And we hear that because it is truth down to the core. That doesn't make it any easier for us—and I can imagine it didn't make it any easier for the disciples—but it is the truth. Jesus told the disciples to wait until the Holy Spirit came upon them to begin their ministry because He knew they would be completely and totally unequipped should they try to start their ministries without it.

God knows the same thing about us and our futures. Sometimes He tells us to wait because He knows we are simply unprepared to do whatever He has planned for us. It is not only a time of waiting—it is a time of preparation. I prayed for God to show me what career He wanted for me for six years. During that time, I got a degree in exercise science and had a full career in the athletic and personal training field, but I still had no idea what my future would look like. I was four years out of college before God directed me to go to seminary. He knew I was not ready to hear that message or follow through with His direction when I first started asking Him during my junior year of college. My six years of waiting was a preparation period that God used to refine me and give me an unquenchable thirst for His Word. When I was ready, He opened the door—and I flew through it.

Sometimes, a period of waiting is necessary because someone else is in his or her time of preparation. Perhaps God wants to place you in a certain person's path so you can befriend him or her, minister to him or her, or maybe even marry him or her—but He knows that the other person is not ready for that step. He throws you into a waiting period in order to catch the other person up so you can fulfill whatever role you are needed in that person's life.

Can you think of a time where God has asked you to wait? What happened when He finally gave you the go-ahead?

The reason we discussed this topic is because it occurred to me that there was a very specific reason why God waited a full week to send the Holy Spirit upon the disciples: volume. Since God knew that every able-bodied Jew would be in Jerusalem to celebrate the Feast of Weeks, He asked them to wait. Then, when every Jew was in Jerusalem, God breathed the Holy Spirit upon the apostles and made it so loud that it drew an immense crowd, filled with Jews who had just traveled from far countries. In turn, each of the people from fifteen different countries had the opportunity to take the gospel and spread it to their families and friends in their own countries and villages. Consequently, the good news of the Messiah spread like wildfire throughout the world.

Sometimes, beloved, God asks you to wait because He knows that at the end of the waiting, you will go forth and change lives, which would not have happened at any earlier point. Trust God in the waiting, enjoy the waiting, and be excited because you know there is a glorious time coming. He knows just the right time.

Week 2: Day 4

Today we pick right back up where we left off yesterday—with our longest passage yet. Buckle up and settle in. We've got some reading to do today! I hope you are starting to realize that praying before you begin your study is one of the most important things you can do to deepen your relationship with God and your understanding of His Word. Never get into the Bible without hitting your knees in prayer first. He is the one who speaks. Always start with an invitation to let Him speak and an open heart that you might hear it. If you haven't done so already, please issue that invitation now. Then open your Bible to Acts 2, and read verses 14–41.

Throughout Acts, Luke depicts Peter as the spokesman for all the apostles. When we read of Peter speaking throughout the book of Acts, know that Luke presupposes that the message Peter shares is with the full support and agreement of the other apostles.

In Acts 2:6–13, the Holy Spirit loudly descended upon the disciples and caused them to speak in tongues, drawing a huge crowd. Some of them were astonished and amazed, and some of them where mocking and accusing the disciples of being drunk. Did you notice how Peter handled the accusers? Look again at verse 15 because we can learn a lesson from how he handled it.

What did Peter say to the accusers?

How much attention did he give to their accusations?

Peter spent *very little time* refuting the accusations of the crowd; he addressed their accusation briefly and moved along. When people denigrate or make fun of you, do not camp on their words. Do not let them pull you from your purpose or discourage you from your God-given goals. Refute them briefly with the truth and move along. Satan wants to trap us. If we stay and argue with those who make fun and discourage us, we will never fulfill our purpose. We will never argue someone to Christ. We love, serve, and pray them to Christ. Do not waste your time arguing with those who denigrate and discourage you. There may be a time when that person comes to you and asks true questions with a seeking heart. That, beloved, is the time to share the gospel of Christ in humility and love.

Have you ever argued with someone about the reality of Christ? If so, what was the outcome?

It is okay to debate with people with a spirit of humility and love, but when emotions are running hot and accusations are thrown, hearts and minds are not open to hearing the truth. They are simply seeking to score points. If someone approaches you and accuses or makes fun of you in your beliefs about Christ, praying for that person is the most powerful thing you can do. Tell them you are there for them if they ever have any actual questions and truly want to learn about your faith and move yourself along. The way you treat someone in the face of an attack is the most powerful testimony you have sometimes. Think long and hard about that the next time you are tempted to prove that God is real by arguing your case with someone who simply wants to prove that He's not.

Once Peter had briefly addressed the accusers, he immediately began quoting the prophet Joel out of Joel 2:28–32 as evidence of the preordained events as they were unfolding. He spoke of the life of Christ, His words, and His wonders, and then he told of Jesus's death and resurrection. In verses 25–28, Peter quotes David's words concerning the coming Savior out of Psalm 16:8–11 as more proof that Jesus is the coming Savior, which was foretold by the prophets and Israel's most favored king.

King David is a foreshadowing of the coming eternal king, the Messiah ben David (Jesus). Jesus was born of the line of David, and He was born in the same town as David. Throughout scripture, Jesus repeatedly refers to Himself as the "Son of Man." Jesse was the father of King David, and his name actually means *man*. David was, for all intents and purposes, the "son of man." There are so many parallels and juicy tidbits that link David and Jesus, but Peter goes on in verses 29–36 to identify the most important thing that *separates* these two: David was a temporary King of Israel. Jesus is the living, eternal King of all creation! As we discussed in our first week, Jesus is the fulfillment of the promise God made to David in 2 Samuel 6:12–13. He is the one who established the throne of David for eternity; Christ alone is the one who sits upon it forever.

In verse 36, Peter tells the Jewish listeners that God made Jesus Lord and Christ and points out that they who this Lord and Christ crucified. Verse 37 says that they were "cut to the heart" by Peter's words.

Has God ever revealed your sins to you in such a way that it cut you to the heart?

Sometimes, it is enough to know that we hurt God to cut us to the heart. More often than not, it is when the consequences of our actions are revealed that we are cut to the heart because of our sins. Many times, we do not understand the extent of the consequences when we make mistakes. Sometimes the consequences are not too bad; conversely, sometimes they change your entire life. What is so astonishing about God is that He reveals to us the depth of our sins so we can see that the depth of His love and forgiveness goes so much deeper. We see how dirty our hearts are or were before Christ, and we are humbled and astonished by the love of God who sent His son to continually wash us anew (John 3:16).

The ones who heard Peter's speech felt the same way as we do when faced with our sins. They were cut to the heart and asked, "What can we do?" Peter tells them to repent, be baptized, and receive the gift of the

Holy Spirit. Throughout Acts—all but one time in Acts 10—Luke shows that in order to receive salvation in Christ, we are to repent, be baptized, and be filled with the Holy Spirit. That's all it takes! The people in Acts 2 acted in their moment of opportunity, and more than three thousand souls accepted Christ as Savior that day.

Week 2: Day 5

Good day to you, beloved one of God! I praise His name that you have stuck through this week's homework and are finishing strong with this last day. I pray that you will be as blessed as I am as you journey through the last few verses of Acts 2. But for now, you know the drill! Get to praying! And then, sweet one, please read Acts 2:42–47.

Can I just say how much I love that the story of Acts 2 does not end with just their salvation?

What four things did the believers devote themselves to in verse 42?

1.

2.

3.

4.

Their acceptance with Christ did not simply stop at forgiveness and baptism. They continued to learn about the one who saved them. They lived in fellowship with other believers, remembered Christ through communion, and prayed daily. We are called to do the same.

Our jobs as believers of Christ do not stop at forgiveness. We are called to be *followers* of Christ. This means we have to know who He was and is, what He did, what He asks us to do, and how to do it. We have to get to know our Savior. We have to read and learn about Him through Bible study and church.

We are to live in fellowship with other believers. Being with other believers benefits us by encouraging us and strengthening our faith through the testimonies of our sisters and brothers in Christ. They help hold us accountable to righteous living, and they help teach us and guide us in our choices and our futures. They also become your family, through whom you have support in every situation.

We are called to remember Christ through communion. This reminds us of Jesus's sacrifice, teaches us not to take His sacrifice for granted, and helps us strive to live up to holiness to which we have been called because of His sacrifice.

Lastly, we are called to pray daily. As believers, praying helps increase our faith by the asking and seeing God answer, and it teaches us what God's voice sounds like. We will never be good at hearing God speak unless we spend time listening and speaking with Him. How can we recognize His voice if we never give Him a chance to speak? If you want to grow in your faith, beloved, put these four things into practice—and just wait for the blessings to pour down from above.

The passage from Acts 2 continues in verse 43 by telling how the apostles continued to do incredible signs and wonders, and awe (fear) came upon every soul. Can you imagine how scary it is to see God work miracles and not know Him as the loving Father that He is? The amount of power the apostles wielded through the Holy Spirit truly inspired awe and fear. We must never forget that God is sovereign and all-powerful.

I just love the words in verse 44: and the believers "were together and lived with all things in common." The word for common in Greek is *koinos,* and it means that all things belonged to the general. They agreed and supported each other in all things, and verse 45 continues to say that they went so far as to sell the things they owned so they could provide for each other.

Describe how you envision this description of the early church:

What might this look like today?

I can't even begin to picture this happening today. It boggles my mind to picture living in a community where God was Lord of everything, where learning of God and praising Him in community was first and foremost in each person's life, where love of each other trumped all quarrels. In my mind, this is but a sliver of what heaven will look like. We are called to love each other like this and give of our blessings to help others in need. Our churches do a great job of fostering this type of giving, but ultimately it is up to you. You have been called to clothe the naked, feed the hungry, and give the thirsty something to drink.[13] Give as you have been called to give, and you will be the one who comes away blessed. It is your heart that will come away overflowing with joy.

Please share a time when God called you to give of yourself to help another and you did. What was the result of your actions, physically and emotionally?

Lastly, I want to call your attention to verse 46; these believers still attended the temple. Like the disciples, these new believers were practicing Jews who did not understand the implications of freedom from the law and daily sacrifice. The temple was much more than a place of worship then; it was more like a community center. They were telling others in the temple of the salvation of Jesus Christ, and the apostles were doing amazing works through the Spirit. "And the Lord added to their number day by day those who were being saved." O Lord, hear our prayer!

Please take a moment to reflect on your journey through Acts 2. What have you learned?

---

[13] Matthew 25:35–40

Did God speak a specific verse or concept to you over the course of your readings?

What questions do you have regarding the events or theology revealed in this chapter?

Thank you so much for persevering through this long and dense chapter! I hope and pray that God has blessed you through your perseverance. I am praying for you every day, beloved.

The grace of our Lord Jesus Christ be with your spirit. Amen (Galatians 6:18).

WEEK 3

Commentary: The Miracle of Healing

Are y'all enjoying the book of Acts? Are you learning something? Acts 2 was so dense; it moved at such a fast pace, and there was so much involved. I know the reading was long and maybe raised some tough theological questions. This week, we get to camp on one particular scene, and it is such a beautiful one. But before we dig into it, you get to hear the story of how God tripped me down the stairs.

I have struggled with back issues since I was twenty-four years old. I had a herniated disc and couldn't have surgery to fix it until I was twenty-nine. During this time, I had two children; Caia was about fifteen months old, and Elli was a newborn. We lived in a three-story townhouse. The girls' bedroom was on the third floor, and the living room was on the second floor. I had gone to physical therapy the day before and tried a new therapy that had me in agony that day. I was praying all morning for God to fix it somehow—just to take the pain away so I could take care of my children. I was in tears all morning, which is seriously abnormal.

Elli was napping upstairs, and Caia was playing in the living room. I heard Elli start crying, and I slowly made my way upstairs. On my way back down, I was on the third stair from the bottom, carrying my newborn baby, when I somehow slipped and went flying through the air. I landed in a perfectly upright position—with my legs straight out in front of me. Since I was carrying Elli, I couldn't use my hands to catch myself. Every bit of the force went straight to my hips as I landed on my bum. For the life of me, I have no idea how I fell or how I landed in that position. I just knew I was going to be in so much pain when I got up.

I checked my baby to make sure she was unharmed, and she was totally fine. I got to my knees and stood up. To my incredible surprise, the fall and landing realigned my hips. I was completely pain-free for the rest of the day! The pain came back, but that was part of God's plan in my life. He used it for my good as well. I am absolutely certain that God tripped me down the stairs and answered my pleas for help that day.

I am sharing this story because we get to camp on the glorious, miraculous, healing hands of God this week. Please turn with me to Acts 3:1–10:

> [1] Now Peter and John were going up to the temple at the hour of prayer, the ninth hour. [2] And a man lame from birth was being carried, whom they laid daily at the gate of the temple that is called the Beautiful Gate to ask alms of those entering the temple. [3] Seeing Peter and John about to go into the temple, he asked to receive alms. [4] And Peter directed his gaze at him, as did John, and said, "Look at us." [5] And he fixed his attention on them, expecting to receive something from them. [6] But Peter said, "I have no silver and gold, but what I do have I give to you. In the name of Jesus Christ of Nazareth, rise up and walk!" [7] And he took him by the right hand and raised him up, and immediately his feet and ankles were made strong. [8] And leaping up he stood and began to walk, and entered the temple with them, walking and leaping and praising God. [9] And all the people saw him walking and praising God, [10] and recognized him as the one who sat at the Beautiful Gate of the temple, asking for alms. And they were filled with wonder and amazement at what had happened to him.

You are going to get sick of me pointing this out, but I am going to continue to reiterate the community the early Christians had with the Jews. I want your thinking about these first few chapters of Acts to be laden with the idea that this was not, in the minds of the apostles, a new religion. To them, it was a new chapter of salvation for the Jewish people of God's covenant with Abraham.

Peter and John (most likely John the apostle) were heading to the temple at around three o'clock in the afternoon to pray. As they were walking to the temple, another man was making his way to the temple gate. That man was being carried. His purpose for going to the temple gate was much different than that of the apostles. He was there to beg for alms for his survival. Verse 2 describes him as lame from birth, which means he could not provide for himself, could not have a family, and would not have been welcomed into community. He was an outcast, and he could not fully participate in temple worship. God told Moses the law in Leviticus 21:17–20:

> Go to Aaron and say: No one of your offspring throughout their generations who has a blemish may approach to offer the food of his God. For no one who has a blemish shall draw near, one who is blind or lame, or one who has a mutilated face or a limb too long, or one who has a broken foot or a broken hand.

Can you imagine being a Jewish person who was not allowed to fully worship God—or a Christian who is suddenly empty of the Holy Spirit because of something completely out of your control? Can you imagine the emptiness, loneliness, and shame this man had to bear for his entire life? He was an outcast and was counted as worthless—a burden to his family. He could not fulfill any of the duties a man was supposed to fulfill during his life. I can't imagine the feelings of worthlessness, guilt, and depression this man felt. He couldn't even fully worship the One who loved him unreservedly. He couldn't enter God's' presence and be reconciled to Him through the daily sacrifice or worship Him as he wanted. Can you imagine the life of darkness this man had to live?

Is there something in your life that is holding you back from entering into God's presence? Do you have unresolved anger or unforgiveness? Are you bound by chains of guilt or shame? Do you blame God for something in your life? Like the lame man, do you feel worthless or unworthy of God's love? Are you an outcast in your family or school? Do you lack dignity and respect that is the birthright of every human being? There is an answer. We simply have to ask.

In verse 3, the lame man *asked* for alms. Do you ask God to heal you—whether your affliction in physical or emotional? Do you ask Him to take the pain? Do you ask Him to break your chains of affliction and replace your shame with peace and dignity? Do you ask Him to show you how to let go of the past and forgive? This man asked the apostles for money, yet he received so much more.

The key to receiving God's healing is found in Peter's reply in verse 4. He says, "Look at us." God tells to look at Him too, especially when we are asking for a miracle (physical, spiritual, or mental). It can be a huge miracle or a small one, but God demands our all. He wants our total and complete focus. God does miracles all the time, and He can do one with or without your focus. When we are focused on Him, we can see and understand the miracle for what it is. When God has our focus, we see ourselves changing from the wicked, earthly person into one with the fruits of the Spirit.[14] We see things as small as birds being fed in the winter or flowers blooming out of season for the miracles they are. When we are totally and utterly focused on God, He gives us the courage and faith to ask for big miracles—miraculous healings, devastated relationships sewn together stronger than ever, and peace in the midst of utter chaos.

We are blessed by seeing God's work when we are focused on Him, but the incredible thing is that we do not have to be totally focused on Him for Him to be totally focused on us. In Genesis 16:13, Hagar is the only person in the Old Testament to name God. Do you know what she names Him? The *El Roi*—the God who sees. He *sees* our brokenness. He is looking at us in our times of need. He knows that if we but look back, He will heal us. Like the lame man, we ask for alms, but the Spirit wants to give so much more.

God does not want to just take your pain, shame, and guilt; He wants to *replace* them! Like the lame man, we ask Him for alms—but God changes our lives. He grows our faith, teaches you the depths of your own strength and endurance, and gives you confidence in yourself and in Him. He shows you who you are and who you can be when you reside in His presence. In the broken times, God knits us back together so much stronger in Him than we have ever been before. When you are going

---

[14] Galatians 5:22–23

through the times of brokenness—be it physical or emotional—thank God for these times and for the work He is going to do within you, even while asking for healing. I just love the verse out of 2 Corinthians 12:9–11:

> But he said to me, "My grace is sufficient for you, for my power is made perfect in weakness." So, I will boast all the more gladly of my weaknesses, so that the power of Christ may dwell in me. Therefore I am content with weaknesses, insults, hardships, persecutions, and calamities for the sake of Christ; for whenever I am weak, then I am strong.

When we are at our weakest, God in us shows the might of His strength. Praise Him for your weakness, for your brokenness, for your heartbreak. Know that this is the time that God is going to show up and show off for you. These are the times when God transforms you! Praise His Holy Name!

Like the lame man, when we ask for alms, we receive life in abundance. Did you notice what he did next? Verse 8 says, "And leaping up he stood and began to walk, and entered the temple with them, walking and leaping and praising God." Can you picture the beauty and joy of this scene? For the first time in his life, this man can walk, run, and leap. He leaps straight into God's temple. The first thing he did was to run into God's presence, telling all who would listen about the incredible miracle God performed through the apostles. When God heals you, what do you do? Do you thank Him and move on? Or, like the lame man, do you dance and praise Him, shouting His glory and wonders from the rooftops to all who will hear?

This man was not only healed of his physical disability—he was spiritually reconciled to God. He was *finally* able to enter God's presence. During my darkest and most broken times, I was finally spiritually reconciled to God. I was raised as a Christian, but things went very wrong for a while. I was very rebellious and became very hard. The whole time God was calling me back, but I refused to let Him take over. I still had too much anger in my life.

When I was in engaged at twenty-one, I finally learned how to be vulnerable and allow another into my life. This person, however, betrayed me. I found myself too broken to put myself back together. I was broken over him, and the trust and faith in myself and my decisions was completely shattered. I could not figure out how to put myself back together. In my brokenness, I kept hearing a phrase running through my head. The voice kept saying, "My bones are in agony. How long, o Lord, how long?"[15]

I looked it up on the Internet and found out it was a psalm. I began to dig through the psalms because the pain David penned on the page spoke to my heart. His brokenness called to my own, and finally I let God back into my life. I was spiritually and emotionally broken, and it took hitting rock bottom for me to give my heart over to God. The moment I did, He began stitching it back together in a way that completely transformed me. His healing gave me a hunger for Him and a powerful love for Him. Like the lame man, I had to be completely broken in order to be restored and spiritually reconciled to God.

God heals us out of His incredible love. He gives to us out of His limitless grace and mercy, but He also does it so that we can share our testimonies with others, tell them of His great power, and validate our words with the proof in our lives. He works miracles within us so we can tell others that God loves us so much that He wants to heal us in our darkest times—and He can do the same for them. Like the lame man, God wants us to share our stories because they hold power! There is nothing as powerful as testament to what God has done for us in our own lives.

If there is an area of brokenness in your life, give it to God. Pray for healing—and be specific. Ask Him to lead you to a section of scripture that speaks to you, reminds you of God's healing power, and gives you hope for healing and excitement about your future. He is the Jehovah Rapha (see appendix 3), and He is calling you to give your brokenness to Him so He can work a miracle of healing in your life.

---

[15] Psalm 6:2

Week 3: Day 1

Welcome to our third week of study! As I write this, I am so excited for the things God is doing in your life—or preparing to do. We have another long reading this week, one in which we may learn a bit, so let's just get to it. As always, please begin your time with prayer. Center yourself in God's presence and open your heart and mind to what He may have to teach you today. And as always, please remember to write down the things God teaches you that you are willing to share during our discussion.

Our theme this week is the miracle of healing. Is there something in your life that needs a miraculous healing from God? Please write it here in dedication to God. Ask Him to give you faith that He *will* work on your behalf. Ask Him for peace from this burden and know that He will provide.

Please open your Bible to Acts 3. We did a fairly thorough examination of Acts 3:1–10 during our teaching time on Wednesday, but I want to revisit those verses. Please read verses 1–10.

Peter is following in Jesus's footsteps by healing all those who need it as they request. However, there is one very important difference: Peter performs the act "in the name of Jesus," whereas Jesus neither invokes God's name nor needs any such words. The miracles themselves were not any different. The difference lies in the necessary elements for the one invoking the act because Jesus was fully God and fully man, whereas Peter was only a man filled *with* God.

In verse 7, Peter helps the man up. The man's ankles and feet are immediately made strong, showing the great power of God at work. In verse 8, we have the result of this incredible miracle: the man leaps and praises God as well.

When God does a miracle on your behalf, how do you react?

Just as we love to see our children shout for joy when gifted with a present, don't you think your heavenly Father wants to see the same from us? He delights to give you that for which you ask—delight Him by seeing His work through faith and praising Him with exuberance!

One very cool thing about this miracle is that it is not just proof of God's power within the disciples; it is also a fulfillment of prophecy. Isaiah 35:6 prophecies about the coming Messiah, saying, "The lame will leap like a deer." This miracle is not an isolated incident; it is part of the grand scheme of God to bring to fulfillment the promises of the Hebrew scriptures in and through Jesus and His followers. The miracle is a fulfillment of prophecy.

I don't know about you, but I am amazed and astounded when I see a prophecy come true. To know that these prophecies were written hundreds, if not thousands, of years before they were fulfilled absolutely *blows my mind.*

Are you impressed by the fulfillment of prophecy?

What thoughts, if any, strike you about God's forethought and revelations in the Old Testament?

I praise God for having a plan and showing His faithfulness to us by fulfilling every single promise He has ever made. In Revelation 19:11, John the Revelator describes his vision of Christ's return on His white horse. He is riding with vengeance in His eyes, ready to reap justice for

His people, and His name is called Faithful and True. He is the only one who will be faithful to you in every promise He has made to you—in His Word and through His Spirit—as He whispers His love to you. I pray that this week He will show you His faithfulness over and over again. Amen.

Week 3: Day 2

After yesterday and the miraculous healing of the lame man, I hope you are simply overflowing with excitement and joy for the work God did in these ancient times and that He is opening your eyes to the work He is doing in your world today. Let's continue where we left off—the men entering the temple. Please seek God in prayer and humility, and then read the rest of chapter 3:11–26.

In verse 12b, Peter asks the crowd why they are putting himself and John on a pedestal and looking as if they have *eusebia*, "holiness." *Eusebia* is a term with which Theophilus would surely have been familiar, and it may suggest Luke wants to make clear from the outset that Peter and the other apostles are not to be seen as "divine men," even though miracles occur through them. Peter teaches them that the crowd's awe should be directed to the LORD, the YHWH of Abraham, Isaac, and Jacob, "our Jewish ancestors."

It is so easy to see men and women of God, especially mentors, teachers, or missionaries, and lift them up to view them as more important than us, holier than us, or closer to God than us. We put these men and women on pedestals and look to them for guidance and leadership. Though we are supposed to seek the council of godly men and women, this verse in Acts 3 reminds us that it is God and God alone who deserves the position of our guide and leader. He is the only one who we can rightfully put on a pedestal of any sort because He is the only one who *will not fail* us.

So many times, we hear about someone's faith faltering or being denied completely because of a teacher or pastor who has publicly slipped into sin: divorced, had an affair, cheated someone of money, the list goes on. We see these people as examples of God in our lives, and when they let us down, we suddenly lose our center and our faith is shaken to the very core. It is so important that we see these men and women of God as regular, sinful people. They have allowed God to inundate their lives, but they are sinful men and women just the same.

You do not have to write any names here, but is there someone in your life who you have put on a pedestal? Why?

As Christians, we need to be on guard that we do not put anyone but God on our pedestals, and we need to strive not to be the cause of doubt in someone else's walk.

What are some ways we cause others to stumble?

What are some ways we can avoid making others stumble?

Peter knew these people were putting him on a pedestal where he did not belong. Consequently, he then goes on to clarify who was truly responsible for healing the lame man: the God of Abraham, Isaac, Jacob; the same God who glorified Jesus, the one whom the Jews killed. He continues in verse 14 to move the Jerusalem Jews by compounding their guilt: they rejected the Holy and Righteous One, insisted on his murder, and requested that a murderer be released in order to do it. The purpose of this language is to bring God's people to the point of repentance by a "shock of recognition" technique and then to open them up to the reception of the restoration and blessings long ago promised to them and available through Christ.[16]

After Peter "shocks" them with his accusations, he bestows words of grace and mercy and calls for their repentance. Also, as is the speech pattern throughout Acts, he quotes Old Testament scripture and prophecy

---

[16] Witherington, *The Acts of the Apostles: A Socio-Rhetorical Commentary*, 188.

to validate the glorification of Jesus and His purpose in the world. I want to draw your attention to v 25–26:

> You are the sons of the prophets and of the covenant that God made with your fathers, saying to Abraham, "And in your offspring shall all the families of the earth be blessed." God, having raised up his servant, sent him to you first, to bless you by turning every one of you from your wickedness.

What do you think Peter meant by this statement?

In week one, we described the prophecies of Genesis 12:3 and 2 Samuel 7; the promises of the eternal throne that would bless all the families of the world. Peter is showing the Jews that the time of worldwide blessing is upon them, but God *still* sent the blessing of Christ to them—the Jews—first. Even though they are the ones to kill God's Son, they are still God's covenant people—and he gives the blessing of salvation through Christ to them first.

Is there any stronger statement of love? John 15:3 says, "Greater love has no one than this, that someone lay down his life for his friends." Jesus took it even a step further; He laid down His life for the ones who actively participated in the taking of His own. He gave His life for the Israelites, and He gave it for you.

Ephesians 1:3–8 tells us that we are blessed, chosen, blameless, predestined, adopted, redeemed, accepted, forgiven, and lavished in grace through the blood of Jesus Christ. You, my dearest one, were chosen by God to be adopted into His family, accepted with forgiveness through grace, redeemed into holiness, and considered blameless. I don't know what you are going through in your life, what your emotions may tell you, but I am telling you right now that God loves you more than you can ever imagine. He gave up His Son so that you could be considered pure and blameless, and there is no place for guilt, shame, or self-doubt when you rest in His arms. Run to Him, give Him your doubt, give Him your fear, and give Him the shame that always seems to creep back in. You are a new creation in Christ, my love. Never doubt it again!

Week 3: Day 3

This is one of the few weeks that we get to examine two chapters in our homework. We are flying through the Word this week. I praise God for your perseverance and pray that He is giving you an insatiable hunger for His Word. Without delay, I ask you to go through your pre-reading time with God and then turn your attention to Acts 4:1–4.

This scene opens up at the end of Peter's speech. As the apostles and the lame man were talking with the people, the priests and captain of the temple and the Sadducees came upon them and arrested them.

Before we get into the events of the arrest, take a look at verse 4: "But many of those who had heard the Word believed, and the number of the men came to about five thousand." Though the enemy tries to stop the spreading of God's Word, it will be heard! Amen! In today's society, where all around the world are those who are murdering Christians, who have illegalized Christianity and the Bible, God has a way of making sure that the message of Christ spreads to those thought to be unreachable. I know you might be in your home by yourself, but can I get an amen? I pray that it blesses your heart today to know that your God is unstoppable!

We are told that the priests, the captain of the temple, and the Sadducees were there, and they were *greatly annoyed* by the things the apostles were teaching. Ben Witherington III says, "Their presence signals to the listener that the issue of power and authority is about to be raised. In short, we see here the beginnings of a power struggle for the hearts of the Jewish people."[17] Isn't that just the crux of human spirituality? There is a power struggle for *your heart* between the adversary and God, which is why Paul gave us the incredible words from Ephesians 6:10–18 (ESV). Please turn your Bible there now and answer these questions.

Why are we to put on the whole armor of God (vv. 11–13)?

---

[17] Witherington, *The Acts of the Apostles: A Socio-Rhetorical Commentary,* 189.

Against what four authorities are our struggles (v. 12)?

1.

2.

3.

4.

Stand firm …

having fastened the _____ (v. 14)

having put on the _____ (v. 14)

as shoes for your feet, having put on the _____

given by the gospel of _____ (v. 15)

in all circumstances, take up the _____ (v. 16)

and take the _____

and the _____,

which is the word of God (v. 17)

_____ at all times in the

Spirit, with all _____ and

_____ (v. 18).

What does Paul tell us is our main defensive weapon against the "flaming darts of the evil one (v. 16)?

What is our one offensive weapon (v. 17)?

We serve the God of all creation, but there is the great adversary who works endlessly to tempt you to stray. He works tirelessly and "is filled with fury, because he knows his time is short" (Revelation 12:12). We are never above falling into Satan's trap; he is looking for weaknesses in our spiritual armor every second of every day. Never let your guard down. Never take off your armor. There is an *enemy* waiting.

In this case, the enemies of the disciples were all closely tied with the temple. The captain of the temple is most likely the *sagan ha-kohanim* who guarded all the priests and watched over all activities that transpired within the temple walls.[18] The Sadducees were the lay aristocracy in Jerusalem and dominated the Jewish power structure during this time. They were most likely related to the leading priestly families and maintained the same ideologies of the priests, including those against early Jewish Christians.[19]

The Sadducees were known specifically for their disbelief in resurrection of any sort, and they most certainly would not have accepted Peter's speech on the resurrected Messiah. Therefore, they quickly put a stop to the preaching by throwing them in prison. It is worth noting, however, that imprisonment in antiquity was not a means of punishment. It was a holding place until a person could be questioned further on the matter. Therefore, when verse 3 says they held them until the next day because of the evening time, it implies that the time for trials had already passed for the day. The men were held until trials commenced the following day.

I pray that God will help you strengthen your armor daily and will show you any chinks so that you might fortify your defense and strike down any flaming darts thrown your way by the evil one. We are at war, dear one. You are in the midst of a fight for your life; do not go into battle unprepared.

---

[18] Ibid.
[19] Ibid.

Week 3: Day 4

I want you to know that I praise God for you and thank Him for His faithfulness in your life. I pray for you and know that God knows your name and sees your struggles and your joy and is at work in both. I am reminded of the words in Daniel 3:18: "And if not ... [God] is still *good! (emphasis added)*" Whatever is going on in your life, remember that no matter what, God is still good! Spend a moment with Him and then please turn with me to Acts 4:5–12 as we continue Peter and John's journey into trial at the hands of the Jewish priest and elders.

Please list all those who gathered for this trial (found in verses 5–6):

This is, for all intents and purposes, the Sanhedrin Council, which Luke mentions in verse 15. The high priest was the head of the council of powerful Jewish temple members. They ask the apostles, "By what power or by why name did you do this?" (They could be referencing the miracle, the speech, or both).

The Jews rightly believed that only God Himself could produce a true miracle—through a prophet—but only by the power of the One and Only True YHWH.[20] That is why they asked Paul and John by whose name the miracle was performed. When Jesus performed miracles, it was assumed that God gave Him the power of the Spirit because He was a prophet. The fact that these men could produce miracles in Jesus's name, however, meant that Jesus was, in fact, God. For the Jews who refused to believe

---

[20] YHWH is the tetragrammaton used by the Jews as the holy name of God. It means "covenant God of Israel." It is not spoken or written by the Jewish people except for one day a year after extensive purification rituals. On this day, when the priest reads the Torah and speaks the name "YHWH," the people close their eyes because in that moment, the glory of God falls upon their faces. Glory be to God!

in Christ's identity as God's Son, this was a huge problem, which they eventually ended up killing the apostles over.

Then, in verse 8, Luke tells us that Peter was filled with the Spirit to make yet another speech. This phrase "filled with the Holy Spirit" is reminiscent of the same power that filled the prophets of old when God gave them a message to speak to the Israelites. Therefore, we again see Peter fulfilling the role of a prophet of God, being prompted and guided by the Spirit in the words he spoke to the council.

The speech you see in verses 8–12 is mostly a reiteration of the speeches Peter made in chapters 2 and 3. It is primarily judicial, using Old Testament prophecy to prove their guilt and Jesus's fulfillment of the Messiah. What is a bit different from Peter's first few speeches and this one, however, is the strong theme of the power struggle. Peter makes it plainly evident that God, far above the council, is sovereign and all-powerful. Some of these men were truly Jewish men of God who wanted to know the truth; others, however, believed in their own self-righteousness and could not fathom that God would save all of humanity instead of only the covenant peoples of Israel.

The problem with prophecy is that mostly, we only have bits and pieces of the whole picture. We can debate exactly what that picture will look like, but when we think we understand the whole picture and refuse to believe it could be different, we usually miss God's picture and the fulfillment of such. When we talk about the future, it is great to have a broad picture of where God is leading us. However, it is pure arrogance to believe that we have it figured out. In all things, we must seek God first and ask Him for wisdom and discernment and revelation of His plan.

Today, Peter's message is still the same: God is *sovereign*. Above all governments, terrorists, powers, social media, bullies, coworkers, bosses, classmates, and friends, we serve a God who is sovereign. He is more powerful than any other power in creation, and He can control them at His whim. One of the reasons I love the Old Testament so much is because this theme is repeated over and over again. God uses foreign kings who do not believe or even *acknowledge* His existence to mete out punishments and blessings in equal measure upon His children, Israel.

King Nebuchadnezzar destroys Jerusalem and the temple and takes the Israelites into exile (Daniel 1), but King Cyrus releases the Israelites to return to Jerusalem and gives them riches and materials in abundance to rebuild their city and their temple (Ezra 1). All of this happens under God's direction!

God still holds the same power over the principalities of earth today. In the midst of the chaos of today's world, I need to know that my God is sovereign. When I hear of the Christians being slaughtered in the Middle East, hundreds of people dying in capsized boats in the Mediterranean, thousands of people dying from earthquakes, and numerous bombings, I need to know that God is at work within all of it. He is using it to bring glory to Himself.

Do you believe that God is sovereign in today's world?

What does His sovereignty mean to you?

I just about couldn't stand it if I didn't know that God has a plan and brings us closer to the fulfillment of it every day. Christ will return and wreak vengeance upon those who serve evil. He will take His throne and mete out His perfect justice upon every person in the history of humanity, and no wrong will go unpunished.

Thank You, Lord, for Your hand of justice, peace, and comfort in the madness of the world.

I hope yesterday's lesson brought you peace and comfort in your day. We are almost through with a very long lesson, and I encourage you and extol you for trucking through it with me! As always, I pray that God gives you an insatiable hunger and love for His Word. Please go to Him with a seeking and open heart and then take the time to finish our week through the words of Acts 4:13–22.

Peter's speech to these aristocrats and temple leaders was bold. It was shocking because Peter appeared in front of these men, speaking like a mighty rhetorical scholar, yet was a common man. These words *uneducated* and *common* have the connotation that they were unlearned in the way of the Law, opposite of a Scribe or priest. Luke is suggesting that, under the inspiration of the Spirit, one can speak like the greatest Greek philosophers and teachers like Socrates (who Theophilus would know and relate). In 13b, the councilmen recognize them as disciples of Jesus; essentially, they are acknowledging that they were cut from the same cloth as Jesus in terms of lack of training and amazing speech.[21]

The problem arises in verses 14–17 when they desire to keep the word of Jesus from spreading, but they can find no grounds on which to prosecute the men. All these people saw the miraculous sign; therefore, it cannot be refuted because, according to the Law, a true miracle could only be done with God's power. They decided to simply warn them (as was custom—the first offense got a warning and the second was prosecuted) and tell them not to speak or teach in the name of Jesus again. I just love the apostles' response: "Whether it is right in the sight of God to listen to you rather than to God, you must judge, for we cannot but speak of what we have seen and heart." Essentially they are saying, "You can tell us what you want us to do, but ultimately we answer to God." This is an idea that not even the priests could argue with. They could not very well undercut God's command to these men! The council threatened them a

---

[21] Witherington, *The Acts of the Apostles: A Socio-Rhetorical Commentary*, 196.

second time in verse 21, but ultimately, they let them go because of all the people who were praising God because of the miracle of the lame man.

Have you ever been in a situation when a person was commanding or urging to do something against God's will? What did you do?

It can be so hard to stand up to someone who is urging you to do something you know is wrong. The person can have a really good argument and be very convincing about why you need to do (or not do) a certain thing. With God's power, we can stand with *boldness* against any person promoting unrighteousness. Ask Him daily to pour His courage and boldness into you so that you may have an abundance of boldness in your moment of need.

Please read verses 23–31. (You can do it! It's the last section for this week!)

After the council's command, the apostles went straight to their Christian brethren and told them all that had happened. Immediately they began to pray, reminding God of His sovereignty above Herod, Pontius Pilate, the Gentiles, and the Israelites, and then they asked for boldness! They prayed that He would hear the threats against them and give them a holy boldness so that they might continue to speak His truth and do signs and wonders in the name of Christ (vv. 24–30). And while they were praying, the whole place was shaken—and they were all baptized in the Holy Spirit so they would have boldness to speak the Word of God.

I asked above what you have done previously when confronted to do something that violated God's will upon your life. Now I ask you what three things the apostles did when confronted with the same situation (vv. 23, 29):

1.

2.

3.

As I see it, the apostles ran to their Christ-following friends, poured their problems upon them, and prayed for *boldness* so they might continue to do the will of God. It's not a hard concept, but it can sometimes be hard for us to put into practice. When the adversary attacks us and tries to draw us into situations outside of God's will—the stakes may even be very, very high—we *must* do three things immediately: run to our Christian friends, pour out our troubles, and pray together for God's courage and boldness to fill us up to overflowing so that we might not fall prey to the schemes of the adversary.

Is there something in your life that you are battling right now?

If so, do you have a Christian confidant who you trust enough to pour out your heart upon and ask for prayer? If not, pray that God will bring you such a person and that He will fortify you to withstand your enemy.

As always, I ask that you write down any concept or scripture that God has spoken into your heart this week:

Lastly, since this week has been about the precious, healing hands of God, do you have a testimony of healing that you might be willing to share (physical, spiritual, or emotional)?

Lord, I bring to You today a heart of praise for the work You are doing in our lives. I rejoice in Your sovereignty and in the rest we can have because You are in control. I praise You because You are the healer of our hearts, our bodies, our relationships, and our minds. You astound me, Lord. You desire our healing and our reconciliation with You. I am forever humbled that You desire a relationship with us and that You desire to dwell within us until we are brought home to You. I thank You for bestowing Your Spirit upon us in our times of need and for filling us with holy boldness to withstand any scheme or persecution in Your name. Lord, I ask now that You continue to work in our lives. I praise You for the miracles I know You are working in and through us every day. Open our eyes to Your work so that we may shout for joy and sing Your praises. You are the Almighty, the Sovereign, the Jehovah-Rapha. In Your most awesome name. Amen.

Thank you for your perseverance this week. I pray that God has whispered new messages into your heart and that you may have a holy boldness to give testimony to the miracles that He has worked in your life.

WEEK 4
Commentary: The Miracle of Freedom

Today, we are going to look at Acts 5 and the subject of imprisonment. Over and over, we will see the apostles and their brothers in Christ being imprisoned, beaten, and killed because of their faith and the choices they made to teach and work signs in the name of Jesus. In America, we don't often have repercussions for our faith. We are seeing a rise of mild persecution, but our lives are still filled with imprisonment. Please turn with me to Acts 5:12–18 (ESV):

> [12] Now many signs and wonders were regularly done among the people by the hands of the apostles. And they were all together in Solomon's portico. [13] None of the rest dared join them, but the people held them in high esteem. [14] And more than ever believers were added to the Lord, multitudes of both men and women, [15] so that they even carried out the sick into the streets and laid them on cots and mats, that as Peter came by at least his shadow might fall on some of them. [16] The people also gathered from the towns around Jerusalem, bringing the sick and those afflicted with unclean spirits, and they were all healed. [17] But the high priest rose up, and all who were with him (that is, the party of the Sadducees), and filled with jealousy [18] they arrested the apostles and put them in the public prison.

As I read verses 17–18, something occurred to me: sometimes we buy into the bondage that holds others. It could be something as simple as buying into the lies of the world. The first thing the world tells us is that we have to look a certain way and have a certain number of things. It feeds us these lies that lead us directly into imprisonment. Women imprison themselves in lives of anorexia, bulimia, plastic surgery, and anxiety. Men are pressed to look buff and stuff, or to have a certain style. God, however, teaches us differently. He tells us that we are *wonderfully* and *fearfully* made in His image.[22] 1 Samuel 16:7 tells us that we are *not* to be concerned with our outward appearance, as the world is, but we must focus on our hearts. That is the only thing God sees. Instead of promoting an outward appearance to please the world, we have to concern ourselves with allowing God to change our hearts into his *imago Dei* (image of God).

We are also hard-pressed to reach a certain level of success. With salaries, houses, cars, clothes, and images, we imprison ourselves with debt and anxiety to keep up with the Joneses and maintain the status quo. Matthew 6:21 says that where our treasure is, our hearts are also. Do you want your heart to be overwhelmed with chasing empty prosperity—or do you want your heart to reflect your Creator? God tells us to give without measure because we know that God provides.

I love the words of Malachi 3:10: "Bring the full tithe into the storehouse, that there may be food in my house. And thereby put me to the test, says the Lord of hosts, if I will not open the windows of heaven for you and pour down for you a blessing until there is no more need." It does not say that you will have everything you ever want. It says that God will provide so that you are not in *need*.

We are blessed monetarily for one reason and one reason only: to *bless others*. If God has given you the ability and the job to make oodles of money, you have been given a mighty responsibility to pour out your blessings upon others, to use your talents to clothe the naked, to feed the hungry, and to help the sick. On the other hand, if you are struggling in a monetary fashion, rejoice! God has given you a distinct opportunity to live by faith and put Him to the test. I once heard a missionary say, "Once you begin to live by faith, it is *impossible* to worry." You have

---

[22] Psalm 139:14.

the incredible opportunity to watch God at *work!* You get to see His miraculous provision. I am not saying it is easy, but God will prove His faithfulness again and again and again. And it is beautiful to see.

Now please continue the narrative found in Acts 5:19–16 (ESV):

> [19] But during the night an angel of the Lord opened the prison doors and brought them out, and said, [20] "God and stand in the temple and speak to the people all the words of this Life." [21] And when they heard this, they entered the temple at daybreak and began to teach. Now when the high priest came, and those who were with him, they called together the council, all the senate of the people of Israel, and sent to the prison to have them brought. [22] But when the officers came, they did not find them in the prison, so they returned and reported, [23] "We found the prison securely locked and the guards standing at the doors, but when we opened them we found no one inside." [24] Now when the captain of the temple and the chief priests heard these words, they were greatly perplexed about them, wondering what this would come to. [25] And someone came and told them "Look! The men whom you put in the prison are standing in the temple and teaching the people." [26] Then the captain with the officers went and brought them, but not by force, for they were afraid of being stoned by the people.

As I read verse 26, I realize there are so many times when we willingly put ourselves in imprisonment: in bad relationships that are physically unhealthy, abusive, or unequally yoked to nonbelievers; in bad friendships to people who use you, denigrate you, discourage you, or pull you away from God; in addictions to pornography (and women I'm talking to you too—smutty books are just as addictive), alcohol, drugs, or gambling. Even after God brought the apostles out of imprisonment, they returned on their own with only a little prodding. Verse 26 says that the priests could not force them to come back, which means the apostles came back willingly. Sometimes, God brings us out of imprisonment—only for us to willingly walk right back in.

Sometimes, however, we are imprisoned by something completely out of our control. It could be something as deep and dark as being abused as a child; you still carry scars that don't seem to heal. It could be abuse in general; maybe you were raped or were trapped in an abusive situation. You are imprisoned by the chains of a past you had no control over.

The most common imprisonments, however, are our emotions. Our feelings are so fickle. We let them lead us astray. In youth, we seek love and think we find it, allowing it to sway our judgment. In sorrow or depression, we let our negative emotions whisper words of defeat in our ears until they block out the truth of God's Word. In fear, we miss out on God-given opportunities.

One of the hardest things to do in life is forgive others and ourselves. I was very, very rebellious as a teenager. I was horrible to my family. I was disrespectful, angry, and hateful toward everyone but my boyfriend and my best friend. I grew up very quickly when I became a single mother at sixteen and through that journey, I began to lose most of my anger and hatred toward others, but I was still very rebellious in other ways. After I came to Christ, I served Him with single-minded devotion, hoping that my good works could start to outweigh my ugly past and that I could finally *feel* forgiven and worthy. Have you heard "East to West" by Casting Crowns? The first verse says,

> Here I am, Lord,
> and I'm drowning in your sea of forgetfulness
> The chains of yesterday surround me
> I yearn for peace and rest
> I don't want to end up where You found me
> And it echoes in my mind, keeps me awake tonight
> I know You've cast my sin as far as the east is from the west
> And I stand before You now as though I've never sinned
> But today I feel like I'm just one mistake away from You
> leaving me this way

This verse was the story of my life for six years. I knew I was saved, but I was bound by my *own* chains of unforgiveness. I was so scared that

God was just one more mistake away from leaving me and that I would forever be stuck as the unworthy, ugly mess I had become.

God always gives us a way out of the mess. In this case, it is the truth we find in scripture. We are forgiven! Micah 7:19 tells us that God casts our sins into the depths of the sea. In Exodus 24:10 and Revelation 4:6; 15:2, there are visions of God's throne that describe an expanse that looks like a sea of glass. God's throne sits in the middle of it. This is quite certain a liberal interpretation, but I like a good picture. It is such a strong visual.

God is sitting on His throne, which just happens to be in the middle of a sea, deep as sapphire and clear as glass. Micah tells us that He casts all our sins to the bottom of the sea. Do you get where I'm going with this? The very second we ask for His forgiveness, He takes that memory of your sins and throws it into the very depths of the sea, which just happens to surround His throne, never to be brought to His mind again. The very second we ask for forgiveness, beloved, we are forgiven. We are purified and considered righteous and holy in His sight.

Like we talked about in week 1, Jesus died on the cross for your sins and to carry the burden of your iniquities. Don't hang yourself on a cross too. It is such an easy concept, but it is incredibly hard to put into practice. I have provided a list of scriptures to remind you of the truth of God's Word (appendix 4). We cannot let our emotions sway our choices; we absolutely must rest on the truth and promises of God's Word. Unlike our fickle emotions, His Word stays true and unchanging! It is alive and active according to Hebrews 4:12, speaking His truth to us in every circumstance.

In the face of Satan's lies, you must repeat God's truth. When confronted with the adversary's accusations, you have to go back to the scripture and tell Satan to flee. You, beloved, are forgiven. You are chosen. You have a God-given destiny that requires you to move past your past failings.

Satan's greatest achievement isn't keeping you from Christ; it is keeping you from your God-given destiny to bring others to Christ. You will never be affective for God's kingdom if you are constantly looking back at your past. The words from the Casting Crowns song above are based on Psalm 103:12: "As far as the east is from the west, so far does he remove our transgressions from us." Honey, God has brought you out of that prison and broken those chains—so get up and get a move on.

Let's continue reading Acts 5:27–42 (ESV):

> ²⁷ And when they had brought them, they set them before the council. And the high priest questioned them, ²⁸ saying, "We strictly charged you not to teach in this name, yet here you have filled Jerusalem with your teaching, and you intend to bring this man's blood upon us." ²⁹ But Peter and the apostles answered, "We must obey God rather than men. ³⁰ The God of our fathers raised Jesus, whom you killed by hanging him on a tree. ³¹ God exalted him at his right hand as leader and Savior, to give repentance to Israel and forgiveness of sins. ³² And we are witnesses to these things, and so it the Holy Spirit, whom God has given to those who obey him." ³³ When they heard this, they were enraged and wanted to kill them. ³⁴ But a Pharisee in the council named Gamaliel, a teacher of the law held in honor by all the people, stood up and gave orders to put the men outside for a little while. ³⁵ And he said to them, "Men of Israel, take care what you are about to do with these men. ³⁶ For before these days Theudas rose up, claiming to be somebody, and a number of men, about four hundred, joined him. He was killed, and all who followed him were dispersed and came to nothing. ³⁷ After him Judas the Galilean rose up in the days of the census and drew away some of the people after him. He too perished, and all who followed him were scattered. ³⁸ So in the present case I tell you, keep away from these men and let them alone, for if this plan this undertaking is of man, it will fail; ³⁹ but if it is of God, you will not be able to overthrow them. You might even be found opposing God!" So they took his advice, ⁴⁰ and when they had called in the apostles, they beat them and charged them not to speak in the name of Jesus, and let them go. ⁴¹ Then they left the presence of the council, rejoicing

that they were counted worthy to suffer dishonor for the name. [42] And every day, in the temple and from house to house, they did not cease teaching and preaching that the Christ is Jesus.

As I read verse 40, something else occurs to me: sometimes in our imprisonment, *we will be beaten*. We will get battered. It will be so hard! The consequences of our imprisonments are so very real. If you are imprisoned by addiction, those addictions will leave you beaten and will possibly destroy your relationships and even take your life. You may be imprisoned by abusive relationships where you are mentally and sometimes physically beaten. You may be imprisoned by fear or unforgiveness that leaves you spiritually beaten. So many times, our imprisonments leave us with scars that run deep.

However, verses 34–42 teach us something else: God always leads us to *freedom*.

Galatians 1:3–5 says, "Grace to you and peace from God our Father and the Lord Jesus Christ, who gave Himself for our sins so that He might rescue us from this present evil age, according to the will of our God and Father." He is our Rescuer! Revelation 19:11 describes our hero riding on a white horse, and He is named Faithful and True. He comes to rescue you from your bondage and break every chain, so that you may live a life of freedom!

Galatians 5:1 MSG says, "Christ has set us free to live a free life. So take your stand! Never again let anyone put a harness of slavery on you." Never again!

Romans 6:14 MSG says, "Sin can't tell you how to live. After all, you're not living under that old tyranny any longer. You're living in the freedom of God." You are free from the bondage of every sin of this world!

Romans 6:18 MSG says, "All your lives you've let sin tell you what to do. But thank God you've started listening to a new master, one whose commands set you free to live openly in his freedom!" His commands set us free! He gives us commands so that we do not have to live *shackled* to the consequences of our actions. He tells us not to have sex outside of marriage so we do not have the anxiety, jealousy, and insecurity that goes with that type of relationship and so we don't have to worry about becoming single parents or catching STDs. God doesn't give us rules because He wants to bind us. He gives us rules to free us from the ugliness that accompanies sin. His commands set us free to a life of freedom.

Galatians 5:13 MSG says, "It is absolutely clear that God has called you to a free life." *One thing* is absolutely clear: God has called you to a life free of the bondage of sin, free of fear, free of anxiety, and free of consequence. Through his Son, we can live in victory. He is calling you to a life of freedom. You simply have to believe it, have faith in God, and repeat the truths of his scripture until you believe them in the depths of your soul. One thing is absolutely clear: God has called you to a life of freedom.

If you are a music lover like me, I am going to ask you to find "Break Every Chain" by Tasha Cobbs. If you don't want to listen to it, at least look up the words. As you listen to or read these powerful lyrics, think about what is imprisoning you today. Ask God to break the chains of your broken past, your addictions, your self-image, your unbelief, and your fears. Listen to the words and pray that God gives you the faith you need to receive the miracle of freedom in His merciful name. Amen!

Week 4: Day 1

Can you believe we are already halfway done? I have been preparing for this study for months, yet now that it is here, it is flying by way too fast. I wish I could sit down and chat with each one of you. I would love to hear how God is working in your lives! I would love to hear your testimony of how God is answering the prayers in your journal like it's a daily planner. For now, however, I will settle for thanking God for the work He is doing and is going to do in your life. Please take a moment to pray before you start looking at Acts 5. Center yourself in God's presence and open yourself to hear His blessed voice as you read His Word today. We are not going to start in chapter 5 quite yet. Please back up just a bit and read Acts 4:32–37.

What a blessed vision of the church. This is a continuation of the early church we studied in Acts 2. It would seem that they are still bound in unity, sharing all possessions so there would not be a single person in need. This section ends with a beautiful example of a man named Barnabas who sells his field and lays it at the apostles' feet.

In all actuality, this was very much a symbolic action. There is no evidence whatsoever that the apostles kept any of this money or used any of it for themselves. It was given to them as symbolic church leaders in dedication to God—with trust that they would distribute it as they saw need. Barnabas's actions in the end of chapter 4 are set up as a positive example of what true giving and compassion in the name of God should look like.

As we turn to chapter 5, however, we see a very different example. Please read 5:1–6.

So what just happened? My goodness! I am pretty sure my first thought upon reading this was, *Good grief. God didn't have to kill the man!* Let's tear this apart and figure it out together.

What kind of scheme was this (circle one)?

Spur of the moment   Carefully planned

Who was in on this plan with Ananias?

What did Ananias do in verse 2?

What do you think it meant that he "laid it at the apostles' feet"?

Upon a simple reading of this, it does not seem like Ananias and his wife did anything wrong. However, the fact that he laid it at Peter's feet was a sign of dedication of a monetary gift to God. Essentially they were trying to play it off like they were freely giving their profit. Just like Barnabas of chapter 4, they were trying to pass off the meager portion of the "gift" as the total sum of the sale instead of just giving to God what was in their hearts to give. It was not wrong of them to keep part of the profit, but it was wrong to try to lie.

In verse 3, we find out that neither God nor Peter was fooled one bit. In this verse, Peter is portrayed as being under the inspiration of the Holy Spirit to see into the hearts of others. Therefore, he immediately knows that Ananias has lied and calls him out on it.

According to verse 3a, what was the first accusation Peter directed toward Ananias?

The first, and therefore primary,[23] sin Ananias made was to let Satan fill his heart and *lie* to the Holy Spirit. Let's take a quick look at what David has to say about trying to hide things from God in Psalm 139:1–6:

> [1] O Lord, you have searched me and known me!
> [2] You know when I sit down and when I rise up;
> you discern my thoughts from afar.
> [3] You search out my path and my lying down
> and are acquainted with all my ways.
> [4] Even before a word is on my tongue,
> behold, O Lord, you know it altogether.
> [5] You hem me in, behind and before,
> and lay your hand upon me.
> [6] Such knowledge is too wonderful for me;
> it is high; I cannot attain it.

What does verse 2 tell us about each thought we have?

There is an ugly part of me that is scared when I read this! I know I have some very ugly thoughts sometimes, and knowing that God knows them before they are even fully formed in my brain is not pleasant. However, who better to transform my thoughts than the One who knows intimately how I think? David gives us a clue about his feelings about God's knowledge in verses 5–6 of this passage.

---

[23] In ancient culture, it was rhetorically correct to list the most import subject first when submitting a list: names, actions, gifts, etc. Therefore, in this case, the first offense Peter lists in the most serious in his eyes. Watch out for this when Luke lists names or actions of people throughout Acts since it may give you a little insight into the person or the situation.

How do you think David feels about God's all-knowing power?

Does knowing David's attitude toward it help give you hope for your own transformation and future?

I love verse 5: "You hem me in, behind and before, and lay your hand upon me." In your present situation, what does verse 5 mean to you?

Thank you for sharing your heart. In every situation, God is your guardian, your guide, and your protection from the things you have put behind you. I won't get too deep into this because we will talk about it later, but I hope you feel the truth of this passage to the depths of your soul. He is cutting the path of your future as well as keeping you from returning to your past. My past is so ugly that this is of the utmost comfort to my spirit; I pray that it is to you as well.

Week 4: Day 2

We left off in the middle of Ananias's story out of Acts 5:1–6 yesterday, and that is where we will pick back up. Please reread this portion of scripture to regain your context and then focus in on verses 3–4.

Ananias lied to Peter (and God) and clearly was not concerned about God knowing his heart, but he obviously should have been. Peter calls him out and lets Ananias know that he has not fooled anyone. He has lied to God, and he has desecrated the sanctity of the ideals of the community in which he lived. He violated the integrity and the holiness in which the new Christian community abided. Peter's words are a reflection of the description of Judas the Betrayer in Luke 22:3: "Then Satan entered into Judas called Iscariot." Peter unveils Ananias's lying heart, and he lumps him together with the betrayer of Jesus Christ.

Do you feel these harsh words are justified? Why or why not?

Dr. Ben Witherington III says, "Luke sees this story not just as being about human greed and duplicitous actions but about an invasion of the community of the Spirit by the powers of darkness, by means of Ananias."[24] The adversary's first objective is to prevent you from entering heaven's gates; his second objective, however, is to prevent those who are already Christ's children from bringing more into Christ's family.

How do you think Satan is trying to "invade" the Christian community today?

---

[24] Witherington, *The Acts of the Apostles: A Socio-Rhetorical Commentary*, 215.

How do you see his work trying to tear apart the church?

How do you think we can prevent Satan's invasion?

How I wish I could hear your answers on this topic! I won't give my own thoughts about this, but I want you see that the issue Peter faced in keeping the newly founded Christian church holy against the schemes of evil are still quite prevalent today. We are imperfect people making an imperfect body of Christ. Praise God for His grace and mercy!

What happened to Ananias according to verse 5?

Yikes. Thank God we don't all end up falling down dead for our transgressions! The literal translation means that he exhaled out his life force and expired. I want to be very clear about this: Peter did not curse or personally kill Ananias. At the very most, this is an example of punitive miracle (a miracle in response to a rule violation). However, the shock of being found out may have caused a heart attack. We do not know what exactly caused his death, but we know that it was in direct relation to his violation against the Holy Spirit and the community in which the Spirit abided. What is interesting, however, is the people's reaction in verse 5b.

What happens to all those who heard of Ananias's fate?

Why do you think they responded with such emotional intensity to Ananias's death?

If I heard about someone falling down dead for what, at first glance, seemed to be a minor offense, I would be pretty darned scared too. Please write Psalm 111:10 here:

What does it mean to you to have "fear of the LORD?"

When you comprehend His incredible power—just how big our God is—how can you not have a touch of fear? Typically, it relates more to being awestruck, but when you understand the raw power at His disposal—especially upon reading a scene like this—how can you not have a little bit of fear? Praise His merciful name that He loves us with an abiding passion and that He only wants what is best for us according to Jeremiah 29:11!

As we return to Ananias' story, what happens to his body according to verse 6?

Did you notice that no one—not even his wife—was notified of his death? They simply wrapped him up and buried him. It doesn't sound like much, but when read in light of the first-century culture where an honorable burial was of great importance, his burial was *highly* unusual.

C. K. Barrett does a phenomenal job of explaining what's happening in this scene:

> When a man had been struck down by the hand of Heaven (as Joshua specifically says was the case with Achan in Joshua 7:25) his corpse must surely be consigned rapidly and silently to the grave. No one should mourn him. The suicide, the rebel against society, the excommunicate, the apostate, and the criminal condemned to death by the Jewish court would be buried ... in haste and without ceremony, and no one might (or need) observe the usual lengthy and troublesome rituals of mourning for him.[25]

There is nothing in the text to indicate that Ananias was a very immoral man; it tells us that he was sucked into the trap of greed. His great sacrilege, however, is the first accusation found in verse 3: the lie to the Holy Spirit. Again, the nature of the sin (greed/money), the entering of Satan into the heart, and the lack of an honorable burial all come together to remind us again of the tie between Ananias and Judas the Betrayer. What a horrible way to be remembered.

Today, the manner of burial may not be quite as important, but the legacy left behind is just as powerful. I want to leave you today thinking about your legacy.

How do you want people to remember you?

What are you willing to do to make that happen?

---

[25] C. K. Barrett, C. K. *Acts*, Vol. 1, International Critical Commentary (MPG Books, 2002) 198.

Week 4: Day 3

This week is a hard week of homework because we are stuck in a chapter full of ugliness. However, it is an important chapter because it shows us how and when Satan first entered the early church. Please take a moment to pray for God's truth to be revealed in your study before we continue reading Acts 5:7–11.

I find it fascinating that Luke gives us a time: three hours later. It is long enough that the men have time to bury Ananias, but it is not enough time for Sapphira to hear about her husband's fate. She wanders up to Peter, and we read in verse 8 that he asks her the exact price of the land. Obviously, Peter already knows how much the land sold for, but he is giving Sapphira a chance to come clean and tell the truth. It is possible that Peter simply wanted to give Sapphira a second chance at coming clean—or he thought that Ananias was the driving force behind the deception and wanted to find out if she was in on the great lie. Either way, Sapphira fails in her opportunity at redemption and receives the shock of her life: Peter was able to see into her heart and knew her deception for the lie it was; but even more than that—her husband was already dead and in the ground (v. 9).

In verse 10, we see that, upon receiving this news, Sapphira falls down dead in the same way as her husband. Like that of her husband, her death is at the very most a punitive miracle and at the very least a heart attack after receiving this shocking news. Either way, Peter did not curse or give judgment on either of these two people; he simply confronted them in their sin and left God to judge their actions.

Immediately after she is carried out and buried beside her husband, word spread of the actions and fate of Ananias and Sapphira. The whole church was filled with fear, according to verse 11. Interestingly enough, this is the first time the word Greek word *ekklesia* (assembly, congregation) is used in the book of Acts. Luke uses this word to show that the followers of Christ saw themselves as a corporate entity; they had become "the church" of Christ. It makes the actions of Ananias and Sapphira seem even worse because they lied to the Holy Spirit and to corporate body of Christ.

This is not just a lesson in lying; it is a lesson of hypocrisy within the church. Luke does not present a perfect picture of the early *ekklesia*; he presents a struggle that began within the infancy stages of the body of Christ and continues within the church today.

What do you consider to be hypocrisy within the church?

Is this something with which you struggle?

Hypocrisy is something we have all dealt with at some point or another. In my life, it has been a struggle—whether it is something as simple as presenting myself as being stronger in my faith than I should be or something darker such as lying to the church and the Holy Spirit about my actions. In my rebellious years, especially as I was cleaning up my act but still not living a holy Christian lifestyle, I was guilty of hypocrisy and twisting the scripture to fit my lifestyle. I could bend the Word of God like Twister until it fit things the way I wanted. I didn't want to change my life to fit to the Word. I tried to change the Word so it fit my life. Lord, have mercy on me! I would tell people that what I was doing was okay because of grace. Actually, that is one of my biggest regrets. I pray that those people to whom I taught faulty theology and twisted scripture did not believe my words and were guided to the streams of truth. God dealt with me in this horribly wrong time of my life—and there was definitely correction—but praise His Holy Name that He is a long-suffering and merciful God.[26]

---

[26] 2 Peter 3:9.

Have you ever run across someone who twisted God's Word to fit his or her lifestyle like I did? How did you handle it?

How do you think we should handle it according to Peter's example in Acts 5:1–11?

As Christians, we are not called to judge. However, we *are* called to confront our brothers and sisters in Christ when they are guilty of hypocrisy and teaching faulty theology. Galatians 6:1 says, "If anyone is caught in any transgression, you who are spiritual should restore him in a spirit of gentleness. Keep watch on yourself, lest you too be tempted."

Please circle the manner of spirit in which Paul says in Galatians 6:1 we are to approach those caught in sin.

Why are we to keep watch on ourselves when we are helping restore another, according to the verse above?

When God calls us to confront fellow Christians about their sins, we are called to do it with love, humility, grace, and gentleness because *not one of us* is above falling into those same sins.

Use the sins of others as warnings in your own life. Take the mistake I shared above and use it as an example of never taking any teacher at his or her word. Job 34:3 says, "For the ear tests words as the tongue tastes food. Let us discern for ourselves what is right; let us learn together what is good." You have to discern if someone's teachings are biblical and true. If someone's teachings about God's Word don't taste right, you have to look it up for yourselves and put it to the test. As Acts 5 teaches us—and as you can see from the example in my own life, hypocrisy runs rampant through the church, including faulty teaching and misrepresentation of living out the Word of God.

I ask you now to pray for God's people, for protection against faulty theology, for discernment, that all hypocrisy will come to light, and that truth will reign supreme throughout God's *ekklesia*. Have mercy on Your church in our failings, O God.

Week 4: Day 4

Yesterday, we finally finished the story of Ananias and Sapphira, moving at a snail's pace. I spent so much time on this short scene because I can see the incredible danger and challenge it still brings to the church today. Every denomination believes something just a little bit different and holds different things to higher importance. If your church claims to be Christian, I don't care what denomination it is, put it to the test of God's Word. Everything we do and believe should be through the filter of scripture. Please spend a moment with God to ask Him to speak to you today and reveal Himself in a new and fresh way.

We read Acts 5:10–11 yesterday during the completion of Sapphira's story, but please read it again. I briefly mentioned verse 11 yesterday, but I want to point out what Luke tells us: all those who heard of Ananias and Sapphire were filled with great fear.

Describe every kind of fear you can think of and how it might relate to God:

The people had a rational fear that was proportionate to the action taken by God. However, I don't think this is the only fear of which this verse is speaking. Proverbs 1:7 declares, "The fear of the Lord is the beginning of knowledge." When you begin to understand the being of YHWH (the Covenant God of Israel), how can you not be a little afraid? We cannot understand Him fully; it is simply impossible for our tiny, mortal brains to conceive His being. However, we can begin to see His power, His sovereignty, and the respect that He demands—and we can begin to learn more about our incredible, powerful, and sovereign Creator.

Has there ever been a time when you have seen evidence of God's power and your spirit trembled with fear and awe of your Creator?

I remember seeing the Rocky Mountains for the first time and wondering at the God who breathed them into existence. I remember looking at the stars, reading that God knows each one of them by name, and being blown away that the same God has yours and my name written in the palm of His hand and has numbered the hairs each of our heads. The power He wields is inconceivable. His holiness is unimaginable. And when you realize just how inconsequential we all are—like a vapor, like a mist—God the Everlasting inspires fear and awe.

Each time we see God at work, we get to see another facet of our Father. The more open our eyes and hearts are to His handiwork, the more He reveals Himself to us. Earlier in the study, we discussed God as the Ancient of Days and Christ upon His return, avenging His people. We should be a little afraid of God—but not for ourselves. We are filled with His Spirit, sealed until that day, and nothing can change that. However, we should be terrified for our friends and family who do not know God as Father and profess Jesus as Christ.

I saw a video of Penn Jillette, half of the Penn and Teller show, speaking about a Christian who gave him a Gideon Bible. Jillette is a well-known professed atheist. One of the things he was saying, however, is that if Christians truly believe in God and that unbelievers will die and spend eternity in this torturous place we call Hell—if they do not tell people and warn them profusely, what kind of Christians are they? What kind of people would let their loved ones go to a horrible place for eternity simply because they were too afraid of being awkward or uncomfortable to tell them?[27]

---

[27] Penn Jillette, "A Gift Of A Bible," YouTube, July 08, 2010. Accessed August 8, 2016. http://youtu.be/6md638smQd8.

Why do you think we are scared to share our faith?

I would love to hear your answers. I feel like Jillette is mostly right; in my life, evangelizing is so uncomfortable because I am scared to offend somebody. This scripture and Jillette's words made me realize that there is nothing as scary as the God of the universe wreaking vengeance upon you. Will our fear of God and His judgment of our unbelieving loved ones trump our fears of the awkward, uncomfortable conversation, of rejection of a beloved friend or family member? That, my dear friend, is the only question that matters.

In the context of Ananias and Sapphira, just like a child should be afraid of the consequences when disobeying a parent, so should we the children of God, be afraid of the consequences of our sins. Even this side of cross, there are *consequences* to our sins. I became a single mother at sixteen years old, and the long-lasting consequences of that sin hurt my son more than me. God forgives our sins the moment we seek forgiveness, but the consequences of our sins remain. The beginning of wisdom is rooted in fear. Revel in God's love for you—but have a little bit of fear because the consequences of your sin may be more than you want to take on.

Week 4: Day 5

This has been a hard and heavy week. One of the things I love about the Bible is that it is not boring. It is gritty, and it is real. What is more real than sin within the church? There are times when I am simply overwhelmed by the harm the church has done in the name of God. We are imperfect people who come together to make an imperfect church. I am relieved to know that this is not a new problem. I love that God is not concerned with outward perception; He cares about the inward conviction of His people. Thank You, God, for not presenting us with false expectations of the early church! Thankfully, today we get to move on from the hard look at Ananias and Sapphira and enjoy the good God was doing in and through His people. With this in mind, I ask you to please read Acts 5:12–14.

The first two visions we get of the early church in chapters 2 and 4 are visions of how they function within themselves. The vision in chapter 5 is how they interact with those outside their community. As I mentioned previously, it is still so vital for the church today to understand how to interact with those outside the church community. Please pray that you may get some insight into how we may better serve those outside our churches.

What were the believers doing inside the church and within the Jewish community, according to verse 12?

As we look at verse 12, notice that the signs and wonders are not specified. We can infer from later in the passage (vv. 15–16) that they were at least healing the sick and casting out demons. These early Christians gathered at Solomon's portico, which was a porch-like section of the temple built specifically so people could gather in community. The temple was so much more than a place of worship in the first century; it was a community center. At that time in church history, Christians were still thought of as a Jewish sect and enjoyed the "perks" that came with this status. Judaism was an officially sanctioned religion in Rome; as long as the Christians were under the umbrella of "Judaism," the Romans could not persecute them. The Jews couldn't kick them out of the community. At this point in Acts, the Christians were still welcome to worship at the temple and enjoy community with their family and friends inside their holy grounds. Verse 12 describes them gathering in worship and performing miracles inside Solomon's portico.

What does verse 13 say about the "rest" of the peoples?

"None of the rest dared to join them, but the people held them in high esteem" (v. 13). This is a fascinating and quite ambiguous piece of scripture. There are two possible meanings:

1. The rest of the non-Christian Jews did not dare to join them because of the fates of Ananias and Sapphira and the resultant fear.

2. The other Christians Jews were scared of the Sanhedrin and did not want to be associated with the apostles and the message of Christ because of the warning of the high priest and council that we first read about in 4:13–21.

Either way, this verse underscores a growing tension around the Christian community—even as they were doing these incredible signs and miracles in the name of Jesus Christ. However, as the text moves into verse 14, Luke tells of the response to the miracles being done: multitudes of people were added to the Lord.

What does it mean to you to be "added to the Lord"?

I love that phrase! When we become Christians, we do not just add our number to a religion statistic—we add our number to belonging to the Lord. What an amazing thought! The moment He becomes ours, we become His—and He never lets us go! Amen!

My translation specifically points out that both men and women were coming to Christ. Again, we see Luke making a point to be all-inclusive. At that point of early church history, Christianity was still being spread only amongst the Jews. Luke still makes a point of including both genders. As we know from the title of this study (*Impartial*), we know that God is pushing the apostles to include those whom their culture would exclude. From the beginning of Acts, and all the way through, we see God's impartiality to the outcast. Blessed be your glorious name!

I love that we get to end our week with such an incredible passage of scripture! Please finish your homework today by reading the rest of Acts 5:14–16.

Verse 14 begins by telling us of the multitudes of men and women who believed in Christ. I have even heard it said that at this point in Jewish history, there were more Jewish believers of Christ than not. All these people began carrying the sick into the streets so they may be healed (v. 15). Luke tells us that Peter was so filled with the Spirit that people thought even his shadow was filled with God's power. They begin to line the sick on the side of the street with hopes that Peter may pass by and the passing of his shadow would heal them. This idea was not uncommon in antiquity.[28] It is not clear if Luke agrees with this concept, but verse 16b indicates that he did.

---

[28] Witherington, *The Acts of the Apostles: A Socio-Rhetorical Commentary*, 227.

This is such a crazy concept to me. What are your thoughts about this?

There is a very clear distinction between God using an object to heal someone and the object itself healing someone. Luke does not say that Peter's shadow was what healed people. Luke indicates that God's Spirit which lived in Peter was pouring out through him—even through his shadow—to heal people. Either way, verse 16 tells us that word got around that these miracles were being done through the apostles and other Christ-followers.

People came from all over Jerusalem and outlying cities to be cured from ailments and dispossessed from demons. Their efforts were rewarded; verse 16b tells us that they were *all* cured. Amazing! I don't know if God would heal people through the shadow of one of His holy and righteous disciples, but I do know that God is all-powerful and sovereign. I will never again say that God cannot do something because studying Acts taught me how arrogant that is. God can do whatever He wants to do—whether I believe in it or not. I am done putting God in a box when it comes to His miraculous power. I pray that, through this study of Acts, you will begin to further believe that miracles are possible and are very much being worked today.

As always, I ask you to reflect on this very long and at times, hard, journey through Acts 5 and write down what God has spoken to you through this material:

Lord, I thank You for loving us enough to leave us in our darkness and sin. I thank You for revealing Yourself to us so that we may continue to grow toward You. I pray for each of us and for Your church so that we may be cleansed of any hypocrisy and live in transparency—with love and humility. I thank You for Your beloved Son who has taken the time to spend with You in Your Word of Acts. I pray that You bless his or her efforts a hundredfold. I praise You. You are holy, You are sovereign, and You are merciful, God. I love You. Amen.

Thank you for your diligence. This difficult lesson forced me to take a hard look at myself. I hope you were challenged as well. During these times of challenge, God is revealing things about ourselves that need some work. His goal is to mold you into the image of Christ. It isn't always easy, but it is so rewarding! Be blessed this week.

WEEK 5
Commentary: The Miracle of Being Chosen

Today we are reading Acts 6, the last chapter dedicated to the first church of Jewish Christians. Please turn with me to Acts 6:1–7:

> [1] Now in these days when the disciples were increasing in number, a complaint by the Hellenists arose against the Hebrews because their widows were being neglected in the daily distribution. [2] And the twelve summoned the full number of the disciples and said, "It is not right that we should give up preaching the word of God to serve tables. [3] Therefore, brothers, pick out from among you seven men of good repute, full of the Spirit and of wisdom, whom we will appoint to this duty. [4] But we will devote ourselves to prayer and to the ministry of the word." [5] And what they said pleased the whole gathering, and they chose Stephen, a man full of faith and of the Holy Spirit, and Philip, and Prochorus, and Nicanor, and Timon, and Parmenas, and Nicolaus, a proselyte of Antioch. [6] These they set before the apostles, and they prayed and laid their hands on them. [7] And the word of God continued to increase, and the number of the disciples multiplied greatly in Jerusalem, and a great many of the priests because obedient to the faith.

This is such a fascinating passage of scripture. I love that Luke does not present us with a perfect picture of the first church. Instead, he gives us a raw, unedited version—one that still had sin and hypocrisy, one where people are neglected—because it gives us hope when we see failings within our own church.

In this passage, the Hellenists (Greek-speaking Jews) were complaining that their widowed women were being neglected and not being fed. It is an issue compounded by the exponential growth of the early church. All of a sudden, there are thousands of sheep to only the twelve shepherds, and the apostles simply cannot take care of them all. The food distribution issue is taking them away from their main purpose, which was spreading the gospel of Christ. Therefore, they simply turn the problem over to the ones with the complaint.

In verse 3, they suggest that the ones wronged pick seven men filled with the Spirit and wisdom, and they will be appointed to help fix the problem. In verse 5, we see that this suggestion was agreed upon by all, and they chose seven: Stephen (a man full of faith and of the Holy Spirit), Philip, Prochorus, Nicanor, Timon, Parmenas, and Nicolaus (a proselyte of Antioch).

As I was reflecting over this passage, a thought occurred to me: these men were chosen by the people because of their relationships with God, but we are chosen by God because He wants a relationship with us!

So many of the passages about being chosen are from the Old Testament, but Galatians 3:29 says, "If you are Christ's, then you are Abraham's offspring, and heirs according to the promise." Therefore, we can take the promises given to Israel and apply them today. The words Isaiah spoke to Israel apply to us as well in 43:10: "'You are my witnesses,' declares the Lord, 'and my servant whom I have chosen, that you may know and believe me and understand that I am He. Before me no god was formed, nor shall there be any after me.'"

We are chosen so that we may *know* and *believe* God!

I love this verse out of Jeremiah 9:23–24:

> Thus says the Lord: "Let not the wise man boast in his wisdom, let not the mighty man boast in his might, let not the rich man boast in his riches, but let him who boasts boast in this, that he understands and knows me,

that I am the LORD who practices steadfast love, justice, and righteousness in the earth. For in these things I delight," declares the LORD.

What does it mean to be chosen? Take a look at the scripture sheet found in appendix 5.

Jeremiah 1:5 says we were consecrated before we were born and appointed prophets to the nations. While God spoke this directly to Jeremiah, we too are consecrated to God and appointed to spread His Word to all nations and peoples of the earth—as Jesus told us in the Great Commission out of Matthew 28.

Deuteronomy 7:6 tells us that we are holy to the Lord, chosen as a *treasured possession*. Ephesians 1 says that we were chosen by Him before the foundation of the world and predestined for adoption into the heavenly family of God. It does not get any clearer than in 1 Thessalonians 1:4: "For we know, brothers and sisters loved by God, that he has chosen you!"

And in 2 Thessalonians 2:13, we were chosen to be saved, to be blessed with eternal life, and spend eternity in the presence of our Lord and Savior. You were chosen before the world was formed. As many times as I hear it, it never fails to bless my heart to know that I was specifically chosen by God to be His daughter. He formed me and consecrated me before I was even born. In the same way, I hope you feel God's incredible love pouring upon you as He says, "I *chose* you." Amen!

As wonderful as that truth is, many of these verses hint at something more. *You are chosen for a purpose!* What is your purpose?

Take a look at Acts 6; the seven were chosen to help distribute food to the Hellenist widows. Up until this chapter, the apostles seemed to be in charge of material distribution within the Christian community. However, now that the community has grown exponentially, it is taking too much time and they cannot focus on spreading the gospel. The seven are chosen by their own people to be the new administrators. They were needed for a specific purpose, and they were chosen to fulfill that role. It is so cool to think that we, too, are chosen out of love so that we can fulfill a specific purpose assigned to us by God. Ephesians 2:10 says, "For we are his workmanship, created in Christ Jesus for good works, which God prepared beforehand, that we should walk in them."

We Christians like to term this as a "calling." However, there is a stigma attached to that word. Most believe that to be called by God is to be called into ministry as a missionary or pastor or some form of full-time career ministry. This idea is very wrong. We are called into ministry, but ministries can be in any situation or career. Os Guinness defines calling as:

> ...the truth that God calls us to himself so decisively that everything we are, everything we do, and everything we have is invested with a special devotion, dynamism, and direction lived out as a response to his summons and service.[29]

There are two parts of being "called." You are called by God as an invitation into His family; upon acceptance of that invitation, you are then called to dedicate every aspect of your life to following and striving to live like Jesus. 1 Peter 2:9 says, "You are a chosen people, a royal priesthood, a holy nation, God's special possession, that you may declare the praises of him who called you out of the darkness into his wonderful light."

Your purpose, your calling, is to live out the gospel message every day; your mission field is the people you encounter every day. God will guide you into the career He has chosen over your life. You do not have to be a pastor, Bible teacher, or missionary to have a ministry.

Think about the most influential people in your life. How many of them are pastors, Bible teachers, or missionaries? In my life, there is maybe one. Mostly, I think of my parents, a couple teachers, and various friends and mentors. These people have taught me and helped shape me and my future—not my lead pastors. It is your job as a parent, teacher, coworker, friend, mentor, or any other role you may fill in another's life to love and serve others right to Jesus's beautiful face.

You are in a unique position to show those around you what it means to love and be loved by God. You must testify to His presence and · faithfulness in your life and the difference He has made in your life. Your

---

[29] Os Guinness, *The Call: Finding and Fulfilling the Central Purpose of Your Life* (Nashville: Word Publishing, 1998) 29.

purpose is to help change people's life—their eternity—by loving them like Jesus does. The Spirit will whisper the invitation into their hearts,[30] but you can help show the way to God through your everyday service and love. Ask God to put a specific person on your heart to show you who needs your love and service the most. When He gives you a name, love and serve them with everything you have. That is the calling of God. He chose us to be faithful to the purpose and task to which He calls us.

Go back with me to Acts 6:3: "Therefore, brothers, pick out from among you seven men of good repute, full of the Spirit and of wisdom, whom we will appoint to this duty." These men were chosen because of their *character—not their ability!*

Philippians 4:19 says, "And my God will supply every need of yours according to his riches in glory in Christ Jesus."

2 Corinthians 9:8 says, "And God is able to bless you abundantly, so that in all things at all times, having all that you need, you will abound in every good work."

God chooses us because of our *character* and our *reliance* upon Him, not because of our abilities. When we lean on Him, He will supply the need. He will give you the ability. Isn't it freeing to know that we don't have to have it all together to be useful to God? I know it is to me! When God puts you in a situation where you don't know what to do, how you are going to do it, or what you are supposed to say, say a quick prayer and rely on Him to give you the ability, wisdom, and discernment in that moment. Like the seven in Acts 6, God chooses to use you in specific circumstances because of your reliance on Him, knowing that He will give you ability in your time of need.

God has called each of us to Himself because of His outrageous love, and He has chosen you to be His hands and feet in this world. You have been created for a specific purpose in this life. God can use you, and He wants to give you the opportunity to be part of His incredible work! What love and what unfathomable ways He has! Rest on Him, let Him build you into the imago Dei, and trust that He will provide the ability. Amen.

---

[30] Revelation 22:17.

Week 5: Day 1

I am very excited to share these two chapters with you this week. In this broken world we live in, the lessons we are about to learn together are supremely important. I ask you to go to the Lord in prayer so that He might speak to you through this passage and open your heart and mind to His word to you today.

Since we covered Acts 6:1–7 in the week 5 commentary. I am not going to spend much time there. I want you to reread it for yourself, however, to remind yourself about what is going on in the text.

Luke makes it very clear that the seven men were chosen for a purpose separate from the twelve apostles. They are "bridge" characters who link the twelve apostles to the next phase of the church. They begin with specific tasks, but they quickly move into teaching, doing great signs and wonders, and debating with the Jewish leaders. Though they are chosen to serve the Hellenist widows, they use their platform to evangelize.

In what ways can you use your current situation or career into which God called you to teach others and spread the gospel?

Please read verse 7 and describe what happened upon the addition of the seven into the church leadership:

Did you notice the last part of verse 7? "And a great many of the priests became obedient to the faith." It was not just the "laypeople" of the Jewish faith who were accepting Christ; the priests were too! We tend to have a bad view of the Jewish leaders of the first-century church, and to be fair, it is not without reason. But like any stereotype, there were many who didn't fit that mold. While many of the Jewish leaders are the root of early Christian persecution, there were many more who had their hearts open to God and saw the truth of Christ. This verse is a great reminder of the danger of stereotyping. As Christians, we know we are to love and offer grace and compassion to all, but it is such a hard thing to put into practice. In all God's wisdom, He inspired Paul to address this issue in Ephesians 4:1–2. Please open your Bibles and read this passage with much intent.

What does Paul ask us to do in the first verse of this passage?

With what characteristics are we supposed to walk (v. 2)?

I love that Paul incorporates using our gifts into this passage! You cannot speak of unity and flourishing within the church without speaking of each member using his or her God-given gifts to bring Him glory. Each member is to use the gifts in the manner in which God has called them; they are to use them with humility, gentleness, patience, and love.

Have you ever been tempted to be prideful of the gifts with which God has generously blessed you? If so, what happened?

I certainly have. God humbled me quickly and decisively. God doesn't allow you to take His glory for long. Not because He's an insecure God, but because He knows that taking glory and building yourself up will destroy both you and your ministry. That is exactly what happened to me. Along with that, my gifts stopped working. I would sit down and try to write or create a teaching, and it would be terrible. Every bit of it would be completely unusable. I have been reading *The Autobiography of George Muller*, and he sums this up so well:

> Neither eloquence nor depth of thought makes a truly great preacher. Only a life of prayer and meditation will render him a vessel ready for the Master's use and fit to be employed in the conversion of sinners and in the edification of the saints … I am glad that I learned the importance of ministering in God's power alone. I can do all things through Christ, but without Him, I can accomplish nothing.[31]

George Muller figured out that pride leads to a reliance on yourself instead of the Holy Spirit. Though Muller is speaking of preaching (because that was his gift), any gift that God has blessed you with only works when it is rooted in the Spirit. Philippians 4:13 says, "I can do all things through Christ who strengthens me." The church, God's people, is at its best when each member is using his or her gifts while resting humbly in the power of the Spirit. Please continue reading the passage in Ephesians 4:3–6.

What are we to be eager to maintain (v. 3)?

Because the Spirit of God lives in us, every label that humans have created to separate each other and give order and control over other humans becomes null and void. The only label that matters is *Imago Dei*: the image of God. You, beloved, were created in the image of God and are filled with the living God. Nothing else any person can say about you or any label they try to slap on you matters: you are the image of the

---

[31] George Muller, *The Autobiography of George Muller* (New Kensington, PA: Whitaker House, 1985) 34–35.

One who created you.[32] You are beautiful,[33] you are holy,[34] and you are a masterpiece formed by God Himself.[35] Each brother and sister in Christ was formed in this same way. God desires that we see the intrinsic worth and dignity of all humans simply because God created them with love and intent in His own image. What stereotype can compare? What label is more important than that?

Please think about and write down the general stereotypes have:

If you cannot think of any, ask God to reveal them to you so that He may refine your thinking so you will see each individual through His eyes instead of ours, which are so quickly clouded.

Please end your time here with a prayer for unity within the church and your community, that God will teach us to see the worth of the individual instead of the stereotype, and that He will give a fierce love for each person simply because he or she is His.

---

[32] Genesis 1:27.
[33] Psalm 139:14.
[34] 1 Corinthians 1:30.
[35] Ephesians 2:10 (NLT).

Week 5: Day 2

In our text yesterday, we saw the church handling problems associated with the exponential growth of the early church. We saw the seven chosen from within their own people (the Hellenists) to help the widows who were being neglected. And we looked to Paul's teachings on how the church should deal with division. Today begins the turning point of the Jewish church; from this point on, we see God working actively to turn His church from focusing solely on converting their fellow Jews to spreading the gospel to all nations as God promised Abraham in Genesis 15. I pray that the material we examine in Acts this week will bless you immensely. Please spend a few moments centering your heart and mind on God and His Word. As we turn to our beloved Word, please read Acts 6:8–16.

In your words, please summarize this section of scripture:

This section begins the passion of Stephen, including the longest speech in the book of Acts. The length and detail Luke gave this event tells us that he saw it as *crucial* to the early church. Luke only had one parchment upon which to write the entire story of the early church; therefore, to spend sixty-seven verses on this one event, the reader understands that this singular event was *vital* to the realization of God's plan for His people.

The passion of Stephen begins in verse 8 with descriptions of his character. What are the three characteristics that Luke names of Stephen?

1.

2.

3.

Luke points out very clearly that he was full of grace and power and was doing great wonders and signs among the people. Luke presents Stephen as standing in a long line of holy figures like Joseph, Moses, the major and minor prophets, and Jesus. Therefore, it is wholly appropriate that someone with such character would be the church's first martyr.

After a reiteration of Stephen's character and the work he was doing among the Jewish community, the focus turns to Stephen's opposition. Because of the miracles that the Spirit was working through him, Stephen becomes the center of attention of men belonging to the synagogue of the Freedmen.[36] Verse 9 tells us that the synagogue was attended by a number of Diaspora Jews from Cyrene, Alexandria, Cilicia, and Asia.[37] The passage tells us that the Diaspora Jews rose up and disputed Stephen over his teachings; however, verse 10 says that they could not withstand the wisdom and the spirit with which he was speaking.

Please look up Luke 12:11–12 and summarize it:

Then look up Luke 21:12-15 and write verse 15 here:

The words of Acts 6:10 mirror Jesus's promises found in the above scriptures in Luke. This is one of the many times we see Jesus's promises fulfilled regarding the outpouring of words defending and promoting the gospel. In this scene, we again see that Stephen is a reflection of Jesus

---

[36] This synagogue was called the "Synagogue of the Freedmen" most likely because it was started by or was attended by "freedmen." Freedmen were former slaves who had been set free by their masters, or it could refer to the sons of former slaves.
[37] Diaspora Jews are Jewish people living outside of Israel.

in the way he lived his life; through him, there is fulfillment of Jesus's promises.

I pray for this to happen in every conversation you and I have with unbelievers! Think of one person who will argue with you for days about your beliefs. No matter what you say, this person refuses to believe. I used to get trapped into these arguments, letting my arrogance and ego lead me into angry debates in which there are no winners, only firmly divided losers.

As I mentioned during the last teaching, we are useful to God when our character reflects Him. Focus on living righteously and pray for an outpouring of His Spirit. He will give you words in these situations. You will be overflowing with humility, love, and servitude. I can promise you that these types of debates will look so much different when devoid of hubris and anger, and though the other person may not be convinced, maybe the divide won't be quite so big. The words God gives you will become seeds left with that person to grow in God's time.

Something struck me as I read verse 11: just because the men couldn't refute Stephen's words did *not* mean they believed him. Sometimes people are hardened and simply refuse to believe—even once they see the truth. We cannot lose hope! Pray unceasingly for the unbelievers God has placed in your life. Have faith that God is at work. He is softening their hearts to one day accept Him as Savior. Your prayers and your willingness to offer Christ to them are incredibly vital. Never stop.

Is there an unbelieving person God has brought into your life and has laid on your heart to witness and pray over? Please do not write names here; instead, use this time to pray for him or her. God will guide you in your actions and words toward this person.

The men persecuting Stephen were very hard in their hearts and they "suborned"[38] men to say, "We have heard him speak blasphemous words against Moses and God." This stirred up the Jewish people and elders; they seized him and took him before the Sanhedrin Council (vv. 11–14). After Stephen was seized, the men set up false witnesses against

---

[38] The Greek word for "suborned" is υπεβαλον and is a very strong word that indicates putting up something or someone in an underhanded or fraudulent manner (Witherington, *The Acts of the Apostles: A Socio-Rhetorical Commentary*, 257).

him. They said, "This man never ceases to speak words against this holy place and the law, for we have heard him say that this Jesus of Nazareth will destroy this place and will change the customs that Moses delivered to us."

Verses 13–14 clarify and repeat the first accusations against Stephen in verse 11. Even while Luke gives us the accusations, he makes it abundantly clear that both the witnesses and testimony against Stephen are false and the actions of the synagogue members were fraudulent and underhanded. Luke reiterates Stephen's innocence against these claims in the last verse of chapter 6: "And gazing at him, all who sat in the council saw that his face was like the face of an angel."

What do you think this verse means?

This scene perfectly reflects the divine character of Stephen. The expression "his face was like the face of an angel (v. 15)," is used to convey "the idea of a person reflecting some of God's glory and character as a result of being close to God and in God's very presence."[39] I can think of another time in Israelite history where a person reflected God's glory.

Please turn to Exodus 34:29–35 and briefly describe what happens here:

Can you imagine being Moses and just taking a stroll up the mountain to have a quick conversation with God? Honestly! What an incredible life Moses lived! For the immediate contextual purposes, however, Luke is indicating to the reader that Stephen is imbued with God's presence and

---

[39] Witherington, *The Acts of the Apostles: A Socio-Rhetorical Commentary,* 259.

is therefore prepared to speak God's Word to His people—much like Moses in Exodus 34.

Have you ever known people who seemed to glow with God's presence? Please describe them, their character, and their ways of interacting. What made them glow?

What were your feelings toward these people?

What steps are you taking to grow in God's presence?

What more can you do to continue your growth?

I don't know about you, but I have immediately loved the few people I have met who glow with God's presence. They are so dear to me and are such incredible mentors and friends. If you have been blessed by knowing someone like this, you have been blessed indeed! We should all strive to be so close to God that we simply seem to glow, almost physically, with His love pouring from our faces.

Week 5: Day 3

Today we get into the meat of Stephen's "trial." What a day we have before us. Please pray that God will speak to you and reveal something new and glorious through our text today. Please turn to chapter 7 and read it *in its entirety*. I know it's a lot, but we absolutely must keep it in context. Bear with me and soak up this narrative history of Israel as Stephen proclaimed it to the Sanhedrin Council. As you read, think of the accusatory context and Stephen's response in light of the false claims.

Did you notice anything unusual for someone who was answering false accusations on a witness stand?

Not once does Stephen refute the false accusations brought against him. He uses the platform he has been given to provide his own true witness instead of addressing false claims. He is not concerned with his life; his only concern is using the short time he is given to speaking the truth of the gospel. O God, that we may be as faithful and as courageous as your servant Stephen.

Before we get into the actual speech, I want to point out some background information. This part of the text is the third event involving the Sanhedrin Council with increasing escalation of results.

Please briefly describe each of these events in the following table:

Passage	Conflict	Result
Acts 4:1–22		
Acts 5:17–41		
Acts 6:8–7:60		

This is the third encounter with the Sanhedrin, and it finally ends in murder. Stephen—an incredible man who is full of the Spirit and so close to God that his face reflects His glory—is killed because of his testimony. You may have noticed that this speech is quite long, beginning with a recounting of Israelite history from Abraham to Solomon, before accusing them of having hard hearts and resisting the Holy Spirit.

This speech is a rhetorical *masterpiece*. As such, it bears at least a brief examination. As 6:12 tells us, the audience was "stirred up" against Stephen. He had to form his speech in such a way that his message would be heard. He does this by establishing *ethos* (rapport with the audience) in verse 2 by identifying the crowd as brothers and fathers and by naming Abraham as "our father." He proves that they have common ground in verses 2b–34 as he recounts the history of the Jews from Abraham to Moses. However, in verse 35, there is a short transition into the *logos* (persuasion) section of the speech. The argument is laid out in verses 36–50. Stephen ends the speech with an emotional appeal (*pathos*), so they may be convicted in their disobedience to God.

I most certainly am not going to pull apart this entire speech, but I want to examine a few things. As I was reading verses 4–5, it occurred to me that Abraham was promised the land of Canaan, but he did not live to see that promise fulfilled. God took him into the land, but he did not claim possession of any of it during his lifetime. Stephen said, "God removed him from there into *this land in which you are now living.*"

There may be promises that God speaks to you that you may not see fulfilled in your lifetime. Like Abraham, God may make a promise to you that won't be completed until you are dust. I just keep thinking of our children and grandchildren. How many family members or offspring do you weep for in prayer, begging God for mercy, that He would soften their hearts and turn them toward Him? We can take comfort in the promise of Romans 8:38–39: "For I am convinced that neither death, nor life, nor angels, nor principalities, nor things present, nor things to come, nor powers, nor height, nor depth, nor any other created thing, will be able to separate us from the love of God, which is in Christ Jesus our Lord."

Stay on your knees and keep praying because as long as your beloved ones have breath in their lungs, God is calling their names and waiting with arms wide open. We may not live to see our prayers and promises fulfilled, but we must have faith that God will remain faithful to His word, even after our spirits have left this mortal realm. Thank You, Jesus.

Are there any promises that God has given you for which you are still waiting for fulfillment?

Thank you for continuing to keep faith in Him and His faithfulness to His promises. God will reward you for your faithfulness. As we see throughout scripture and in our own lives, He *always* keeps His promises!

Week 5: Day 4

Yesterday you read all of Stephen's speech to the Sanhedrin Council, but we didn't get to examine much of it. Today, we continue to pull apart the sermon recounting Israel's history. Please familiarize yourself with the speech and skim back over Acts 7—with the prayer that God may speak anew to you today.

As you continue to examine Stephen's speech and recounting of Israelite history, you may notice that he quotes many scripture verses. Some say there are ten or more, but I found eight explicit references, which I have included in the chart below. If you'd like to, please spend some time verifying these citations on your own.

Passage in Acts 7	Scripture Cited
v. 3	Genesis 12:1
vv. 6–7	Genesis 15:13–14
vv. 26–29	Exodus 2:13–14
v. 32	Exodus 3:6
v. 37	Deuteronomy 18:15
v. 40	Exodus 32:1,23
vv. 42b–43	Amos 5:25–27
vv. 49–50	Isaiah 66:1–2

However, there is one verse that caused me a bit of confusion. If you will, please turn your attention to Acts 7:25. As I read this, I could not find this reference for the life of me! Finally, I found in one of my commentaries that I could not find the reference because it is not actually mentioned anywhere in the Old Testament.

According to Dr. Witherington, it is an editorial comment that reflects the personal beliefs of Stephen (and the author).[40] It is one of the few comments in which we see the personal theology of the speaker,

---

[40] Witherington, *The Acts of the Apostles: A Socio-Rhetorical Commentary,* 269.

and possibly Jewish tradition, shining through the historical accounting. Stephen believes that Moses killed the Egyptian with the thinking that his Jewish brethren would understand that he was chosen by God to rescue them, but they did not. It is possible that Stephen included it as justification for the murder Moses committed. I don't know that there is any application to this little tidbit of information, but I found it interesting that Stephen included this small bit of commentary into his historical accounting.

As we have previously discussed, Stephen is presented as being part of a long line of Israelite prophets. This idea is also reflected in his speech as he follows the pattern of prophets in calling out the sins of the people (c.f. 2 Kings 17:7–20; Nehemiah 9:26; 2 Chronicles 36:14–16). After he lays the foundation of his argument, he finally gets to the heart of the matter in verse 51. They are stiff-necked or stubborn people, they are uncircumcised in their hearts and ears (they are spiritually dead and refuse to hear the truth), and they are always resistant to the Holy Spirit. He ties the accusation back to the history he previously gave and shows that they are acting exactly like their ancestors.

We are so quick to judge the ancient Jews and scoff at their hard hearts, but I wonder if I would have reacted any differently?

Have there been times in your life when you were too stubborn to see the truth until God had to press it upon you—maybe in unpleasant ways?

I know that I have. Many times! God and I have had a rough couple of years dealing with my pride and ego, especially my know-it-all attitude. He knew that, in order for me to be any kind of leader for Him, we had to deal with my issues first.

Have you ever had a time of refinement where you felt God was working something out within you? What was it?

What did He use to rid you of it?

Was there a specific purpose or reason for your period of refinement?

I praise Him for His incredible grace and mercy! I am so grateful that He loves us too much to leave us in our sin. He is constantly working within us to rid us of our ugliness and fill us with His beauty. Praise His holy name!

Today, we finally finish with Stephen's story. We are going to dive right in—after your prayer time, of course. Please reread the remainder of 7:54–60.

As you look at verse 54, what was the crowd's reaction?

Although the crowd was very angry at Stephen's words, it is not until he utters the next phrase in verse 56 that they are enraged and stone him. Up until that point, they are fully convicted—and no one likes it when someone points out their failings—but they are not murderous.

This next verse is so beautiful: "But he, full of the Holy Spirit, gazed into heaven and saw the glory of God, and Jesus standing at the right hand of God" (v. 55). The meaning of Jesus standing at the right hand of God is somewhat debated, but most likely, this is reflective of Jesus's words in Luke 12:8: "And I tell you, everyone who acknowledges me before men, the Son of Man also will acknowledge before the angels of God." Stephen sees Jesus in His legal role in heaven, witnessing before God that Stephen is one of His. I just love this! Jesus is standing there at God's right hand, pointing at us in our brightest moments, and saying, "Look at that person right there. That one is mine!"

How does it make you feel to know that Jesus is witnessing for you in heaven?

It makes me so very joyous—but also quite scared. I don't want to let Him down. At the end of my life, I want to hear Him say, "Well done, my good and faithful servant!"[41] I pray that we each will have the strength and conviction to run our races well.[42]

After Stephen sees Jesus, he proclaims what he is seeing in verse 56. After his declaration, the people stone him, which indicates they believe they have heard blasphemy. To these Jewish men, the idea that a mortal man, even a prophet, would stand at the right hand of YHWH was unthinkable. Therefore, they covered their ears to prevent hearing anything more, rushed together, and took him outside the city to stone him. Verse 58 tells us that the witnesses of Stephen's murder laid down their garments at the feet of a young man named Saul.

Just who do you think this man named Saul is?

He is Saul of Tarsus, the one who becomes Paul, the great apostle to the Gentiles. He is the one overseeing the stoning of Stephen. Scripture *never once* indicates that the Sanhedrin Council pronounced Stephen guilty. The *people* pronounced judgment upon him in their anger. The Jewish *people* fell upon him without official conviction and stoned him to death.

Please take a look at verses 59–60; do Stephen's last words remind you of anything?

As I said before, Stephen is presented as being in the line of Jesus. There are ten parallels between the passions of Stephen and Jesus:[43]

---

[41] Matthew 25:21.

[42] 1 Corinthians 9:24.

[43] Witherington, *The Acts of the Apostles: A Socio-Rhetorical Commentary,* 253.

Parallel	Jesus	Stephen
Trial before the high priest/ Sanhedrin	Mark 14:53	Acts 6:12; 7:1
False witnesses	Mark 14:56–57; Matthew 26:60–61	Acts 6:13
Testimony of the destruction of the temple	Mark 14:58; Matthew 26:61	Acts 6:14
Temple "made with hands"	Mark 14:58	Acts 7:56
Son of Man saying	Mark 14:62	Acts 7:56
Charge of blasphemy	Mark 14:64; Matthew 26:63	Acts 6:11
High priest's question	Mark 14:61; Matthew 26:63	Acts 7:1
Committal of spirit	Luke 23:46	Acts 7:59
Cry out with a loud voice	Mark 15:34; Mark 15:37; Matthew 27:46	Acts 7:60
Intercession for enemies' forgiveness	Luke 23:34	Acts 7:60

What significance, if any, do you think is conveyed by these parallels?

To be quite honest, I do not know. I found it to be awfully fitting, however, that the first martyr after Christ's ascension would parallel Jesus's own martyrdom so clearly. Stephen is shown to be so full of the Spirit—and so close to God—that he physically reflected God's glory. I cannot believe it is coincidence that his death so closely followed the pattern of Jesus's death.

This passage is such a heavy one. Stephen was the first to die for his faith, but he will certainly not be the last. His death, however, pushed the Christians out of Jerusalem and into other areas of Israel. After this chapter, we will see Christianity starting to branch out from its Jewish roots and begin to fulfill the words Jesus last spoke to the apostles: "You will be my witnesses into Judea and Samaria, unto all the ends of the earth (Acts 1:8)." God takes the ugly and turns it into something beautiful. This scene is certainly ugly, but God uses it to start spreading the gospel message to the rest of the world. What is more beautiful than that?

What did God speak to you through His Word this week?

Do you have any questions regarding the passion of Stephen?

Thank you, beloved, for persevering through Acts 6 and 7 with me. I know it got a little scholarly and technical at times, but I hope God spoke to you through the reading of His Word and blessed you through it.

Dearest Lord, I thank You for this person who makes You a priority in his or her life and chooses to spend time with You and learn about You. I praise You because You are constantly teaching us and transforming us into Your image. I pray that You continue to mold us into Your image, O God. Thank You for Your Word to us this week. Thank You for Your guidance and Your love. In Your most holy name, I pray. Amen.

WEEK 6
Commentary: A Lesson in Refinement

In your reading and discussion of week 5, we examined Stephen's martyrdom and was introduced to a man named Saul. In this context, we open to Acts 8:1–3:

> [1] And Saul approved of his execution. And there arose on that day a great persecution against the church in Jerusalem, and they were all scattered throughout the regions of Judea and Samaria, except the apostles. [2] Devout men buried Stephen and made great lamentation over him. [3] But Saul was ravaging the church, and entering house after house, he dragged off men and women and committed them to prison.

We will discuss this section much more in your homework this week, but it is important to gain some context through these few verses. Saul oversaw the stoning of Stephen, and once the first martyr was executed, it was like he unleashed his own personal war against the Jewish Christians. He approved of Stephen's execution, and we see the savagery and single-minded focus he had in verse 3. Saul was ravaging the church, entering house after house, dragging off men and women, and throwing them in prison. He was taking it upon himself to rid Jerusalem of this—in his mind—blasphemous sect.

We tend to vilify those Jews who persecuted the Christians, but those Jews—though their ears and hearts were closed to God's truth—were told by God through Moses in Leviticus 24:16 that, "Whoever blasphemes the name of the LORD shall surely be put to death. All the congregation shall stone him. The sojourner as well as the native, when he blasphemes the Name, shall be put to death."

Saul and the other Jews did not understand that Jesus fulfilled the Law of Moses and instituted the new covenant in His blood. In their refusal to hear, they clung to the old ways and persecuted those who they thought were blaspheming God. This single-minded persecution led by Saul scatters the church throughout the regions of Judea and Samaria, all except the apostles (verse 1). Stephen's martyrdom was part of a bigger plan. It was the beginning of the fulfillment of Jesus's directive to reach the ends of the world with the gospel message. Stephen's death opened the doors of salvation for the rest of the world. In this context, we turn to Philip's story. Please turn with me to read verses 4–8:

> [4] Now those who were scattered went about preaching the word. [5] Philip went down to the city of Samaria and proclaimed to them the Christ. [6] And the crowds with one accord paid attention to what was being said by Philip when they heard him and saw the signs that he did. [7] For unclean spirits, crying out with a loud voice, came out of many who had them, and many who were paralyzed or lame were healed. [8] So there was much joy in that city.

Philip was one of the Greek Jews chosen by the Greek-speaking Jewish widows in chapter 6. When we first meet Philip, he was picked to serve the widows food, but—like Stephen—we soon see him teaching by himself in a new place and doing incredible signs! In this man, we can see the evolution of ministry as a Christian.

God does not expect you to become a Christian and immediately begin teaching others. Unless you feel God calling you to a specific place, sometimes figuring where and how to serve Him can be a conundrum. Philip shows us that you can start small. Pick a task-based service and begin there. Find something you feel comfortable with: handing out bulletins, being on the tech team, helping people park their cars, or opening the doors for people. Every single service that you provide in the name of God is important, and God will bless you for it. Who knows how He will grow you and what He will grow you into just by taking that first little step. Philip began as a food server and ended up as a missionary in Samaria.

I find it fascinating that God chose Philip—a Greek Jew—to go to Samaria. The Samaritans claimed to be of the line of Abraham—and therefore heirs according to God's covenant with Abraham. They studied a version of the Pentateuch, the first five books of the OT attributed to authorship by Moses. When they intermarried with other kingdoms and became impure (according to Deuteronomic Law), the Jewish people rejected them.

In Ezra 4, the Samaritans offered to help rebuild the temple with the exiles who came out of Babylon, but their offer was rejected because of their impurity. They became embittered and worked with other peoples of the land to stop the building of the temple. They were successful for about fourteen years before Nehemiah came along and led the Jews to finish it. Therefore, there was mutual animosity between the two kingdoms that festered and bubbled with hatred.

I wonder if God knew the animosity between the Jerusalem Jews and the Samaritans was so strong that the apostles would not have been able to breach the barriers of their own ethnicity and culture. Did God send Philip—a Greek Jew—instead? The Greek-speaking Jews were seen as being a little less than the Jews from Israel. Philip shared in the "outside" status of the Samaritans because of his origins. It is possible that Philip had more in common with the Samaritans than the apostles, and was therefore better able to communicate with them.

In Acts 8, we first see evidence that the gospel message is being pushed out of Jerusalem toward the people who the Jews believed were unclean. Philip—who was not an apostle—was willing to spread the message to these unclean peoples. We are told in this short section that he was proclaiming Christ to them, and they were paying attention to him "with one accord," hearing his message, and seeing the signs that he was doing. "There was so much joy in that city." Doesn't that reaction kind of sum it up? Where there is the gospel, there is joy!

But there is much more to this story. Continue with verses 9–13:

⁹ But there was a man named Simon, who had previously practiced magic in the city and amazed the people of Samaria, saying that he himself was somebody great. ¹⁰ They all paid attention to him, from the least to the greatest, saying, "This man is the power of God that is called Great." ¹¹ And they paid attention to him because for a long time he had amazed them with his magic. ¹² But when they believed Philip as he preached good news about the kingdom of God and the name of Jesus Christ, they were baptized, both men and women. ¹³ Even Simon himself believed, and after being baptized he continued with Philip. And seeing signs and great miracles performed, he was amazed.

There is a great magician named Simon who, according to verse 9, said "that he himself was somebody great."

We are seeing a direct contrast between Simon and Philip. I love what one of my commentaries said about Philip and his work of miracles within Samaria: "Luke calls these works signs, for he sees them as pointing beyond themselves as confirmation of the message, which is more critical."[44] Philip used signs to confirm and point to the truth and power of God. The first thing we hear about Simon is that he calls himself someone great. Simon was playing with magic to raise himself up; Philip was relying on the power of God to confirm the message of the gospel.

In verse 10, the people paid attention to Simon because of his magic. They said, "This man is the power of God that is called Great." This specific title is an interesting one because there is inscriptional evidence in historical documents of Samaria of a "lesser god" they called "the Great Power." The Samaritans could have been referencing this lesser god.

In verse 6, the crowds were paying attention to Philip's message, and in verse 10, the peoples were paying attention to Simon's message. Therefore, Luke set up a contrast between Philip and Simon in which they are in competition for the people's attention. We are not told what

---

44 Witherington, *The Acts of the Apostles: A Socio-Rhetorical Commentary*, 283.

kind of magic Simon performs, but it obviously could not compete with the signs Philip was doing within the city.

In verse 12, the people believed Philip about the kingdom of God and the name of Jesus Christ, and they were baptized. In verse 13, Luke tells us that even Simon believed and was baptized because of the great signs and miracles Philip performed. Did you notice what was missing from all these conversions? Luke never mentions the baptism of the Holy Spirit. I have previously mentioned that conversion from Luke almost always has a three-pronged element: belief, baptism by water, and baptism by the Holy Spirit. We have yet to see it here. Turn with me to verses 14–17:

> [14] Now when the apostles at Jerusalem heard that Samaria had received the word of God, they sent to them Peter and John, [15] who came down and prayed for them that they might receive the Holy Spirit, [16] for he had not yet fallen on any of them, but they had only been baptized in the name of the Lord Jesus. [17] Then they laid their hands on them and they received the Holy Spirit.

This is such a delightful little piece of scripture. Some speculate that the apostles came to Samaria because they simply could not believe the dreaded Samaritans were accepting the gospel. Others think they came to celebrate with them. I think God was pushing the limits of their understanding because, though Jesus told them in Acts 1:8 to take the gospel to the rest of the world, I don't think they understood it was for the Gentiles of the world. The Samaritans weren't quite considered Gentiles, and the Jews reviled them for the way they "tainted" Jewish purity. I think God was stretching their understanding of the gospel, and they had to have confirmation with their own eyes that it was happening.

We see the first miracle of transformation within the apostles and the first Christians. God is constantly shaping our understanding of Him and who He is, and He is changing our hearts to reflect Him. I cannot imagine that it would be any different back then!

This week, we are reminded through the transformation of the minds and hearts of the apostles that our hearts, minds, attitudes, emotions, and relationships are being constantly transformed. We are transformed into His beautiful image (see appendix 6).

Sometimes, like the apostles in this section, we embrace transformation. We welcome God to teach us, expand our understanding, and change our perspective. One of my readings made a really cool parallel to the apostle John we meet in Acts 8 in contrast to his younger self in Luke 9:54. If you will, turn with me to Luke 9:51–55:

> [51] When the days drew near for [Jesus] to be taken up, he set his face to go to Jerusalem. [52] And he sent messengers ahead of him, who went and entered a village of the Samaritans, to make preparations for him. [53] But the people did not receive him, because his face was set toward Jerusalem. [54] And when his disciples James and John saw it, they said, "Lord, do you want us to tell fire to come down from heaven and consume them?" [55] But he turned and rebuked them. [56] And they went on to another village.

Conrad Gempf says, "It is, of course, delightful that John, who once wanted to call down the fire of judgment on a Samaritan village (Luke 9:54), was one of those who was now calling down the Holy Spirit."[45]

God changed John's heart of judgment and readiness to dispense His own brand of justice on the Samaritans to a heart ready to bless these same people by praying upon them and calling the Holy Spirit to baptize them with His grace and power. This is one beautiful example in the New Testament of God transforming people into His image.

However, sometimes we resist transformation. Let's take a look at the rest of the scene in Acts 8:18–24:

> [18] Now when Simon saw that the Spirit was given through the laying on of the apostles' hands, he offered them money, [19] saying, "Give me this power also, so that

---

[45] Conrad Gempf, "Acts," in *New Bible Commentary*, Twenty-First Century edition, edited by G. J Wenham, et. al. (Downers Grove, IL: InterVarsity Press, 1994), 1079.

anyone on whom I lay my hands may receive the Holy Spirit." [20] But Peter said to him, "May your silver perish with you, because you thought you could obtain the gift of God with money! [21] You have neither part nor lot in this matter, for your heart is not right before God. [22] Repent, therefore, of this wickedness of yours, and pray to the Lord that, if possible, the intent of your heart may be forgiven you. [23] For I see that you are in the gall of bitterness and in the bond of iniquity." [24] And Simon answered, "Pray for me to the Lord, that nothing of what you have said may come upon me."

Peter is blessed with the gift of seeing into people's heart and knowing their intentions. In his heart, Simon wanted the gift of the Holy Spirit so he could amaze people, and Peter called him out on it. Simon desired the power of the Holy Spirit more than he wanted the Spirit itself. His one desire was not to spread the glory of God—it was to spread the glory of himself.

I feel like we all struggle with at least one thing. Pride is definitely one of my things. About two years ago, God said, "Girl, we gotta get this pride thing under control!" We got to work, but I did not want to let go of my pride. It was ugly. Pride got me through being a single mother in high school—and a lot of other things—before I was reliant on God. Pride drove me to overcome the obstacles life threw at me. It was how I knew how to fight! I think of "Overcomer" by Mandisa, and I definitely thought of myself as an overcomer—by my own power.

To overcome the things in my past, I drove myself to exhaustion. I had panic attacks, constant migraines and my body shut down. I had to have surgery because of the stress I put on myself to overcome. My pride drove me to not give up. A good type of pride drives you to do your best, but I became a slave to it. I was killing myself because of my pride.

When God began to work it out of me, I was not happy about it. It was a two-year struggle where God drove me to scripture after scripture and study after study that told me of the failings of pride. He showed me the consequences of pride in my own life. He showed me very clearly when I was starting to glorify myself instead of Him. Finally, He told me to get on my face before Him when I prayed. I had always heard of doing this, but I thought it was ridiculous. I would tell myself that I could pray just as well while sitting nice and comfortable in my chair as I could on my stomach on the floor.

God showed me that my refusal to get on the floor in front of Him was because I was too proud to bow before anything or anyone, including Him. I could submit my will to Him, but there is something about taking up a physical position of submission that changes your thinking. It reinforces submission to Him in every single way.

When I began to pray from the floor, I truly began to let go of my pride and fully submitted to Him. Two years later, it is still a struggle. I still struggle with glorifying myself instead of Him. I daily struggle with pride, but it has become easier to give up. It is easier to recognize, and it is easier to give it back to God. God has changed many other things in my heart, but this one has been the hardest. I have fought the hardest, and it has taken the longest. God knew I had to give up my pride and self-glorification before I could succeed in the works He had prepared for me. He knew I would be of no use to Him if my eyes were on myself.

Simon refused to give up his own glorification and his own pride. Notice his last words to the apostles in verse 24: "Pray for me to the Lord, that nothing of what you have said may come upon me." Even after Peter's words to him, Simon wanted to escape the consequences of his evil ways. He did not want to change his ways. He just wanted to avoid the consequences of it.

We often see the consequences after it is too late to change. God does not want that for us. He calls us to submit to Him so He can transform us into His image and have hope for our future without fearing the consequences of our wicked ways.

What do you struggle with? Is God telling you it is time to change something in your life? There is always something. Philippians 1:6 tells us that God is working on us until Christ returns in glory, but some things are harder than others to give up.

> And we all, with unveiled faces, beholding the glory of
> the Lord, are being transformed into the same image

from one degree of glory to another. For this comes from
the Lord who is the Spirit. (2 Corinthians 3:18)

Go to God with an unveiled face, and allow Him to transform you
into the imago Dei so you may reflect He who made you and live a life
full of joy and hope.

Week 6: Day 1

Good day to you! I am sitting in shock and wonder at the fact that we only have two weeks left of our study. I pray that God is at work in you through this study and that He is teaching you about Himself and who you are in Him. I am feeling very humbled tonight. The rains have stopped, and the most beautiful sky is glowing through my window. God created such magnificence, and He chooses to raise us up over all of it, crowning us in glory in honor.[46] How can we not be humbled when faced with such wonder?

With these words in your mind, please turn to the Lord and praise Him for being such an incredible and awesome God. Ask Him to open your mind and heart to the things He has to teach you through this chapter.

I won't go into much detail regarding the story between Philip and Simon, but I want to say a couple of words about Saul's part in Acts 8:1–3. Please refresh these verses in your memory and reread them.

Before this chapter, the early Christians encountered some opposition by the Jews, but they were able to come together with relative freedom from the Jews and the Roman Empire because they were still recognized as a sect of Judaism. Since the Roman Empire recognized Judaism as a religion, they had the freedom to practice their religion without persecution.

In the first few verses of chapter 8, we begin to see that freedom crumbling. Once the Jews began to actively purge the Jewish Christians from their temples and denounce the Christians as a Jewish "sect," the Christians faced persecution from both the Jews and the Roman Empire. In the first verses of Acts 8, we hear whispers of the impending terror waged against the early Christians.

What is the tone of vv. 1–3?

---

[46] Psalm 8:3–5.

Can't you hear the urgency and the single-minded focus of Saul as he purged Jerusalem of the Christians? Luke wanted to convey the savagery of Saul's persecution of the Christians so that we might have a greater understanding of the miracle of his conversion to Christianity in the following chapter. He was teaching us that Saul was a violent zealot who seemed to have no mercy. His heart was very hard, and he was only mindful of the Law—and not of God. He had lost sight of the love upon which the Law was built.

The Shema was the centerpiece of the morning and evening prayer services in Jewish religion. The first words of the Shema are found in Deuteronomy 6:4–5: "Hear, O Israel: The Lord our God, the Lord is one. You shall love the Lord your God with all your heart and with all your soul and with all your might." Even though Saul prayed this prayer at least twice a day, he forgot to live it. He had forgotten his first love,[47] and he replaced God's position with the Law. O, how we do the same.

Have you forgotten your first love? Have you made it your practice to love God with all your heart, soul and might? Do you love others because the God whom you love lives within them?

How many times have we judged and turned someone away when we should have loved? How many times have we thought of someone as unworthy of our time—even something as simple as hanging up on a telemarketer! I used to do that all the time until my brother's best friend worked for one. Within two weeks, he was depressed. Within a couple months, he was suicidal. Obviously, there were underlying issues, but the way he was talked to and treated by everyone on the phone for eight hours a day compounded the issues. Lucky for us, he was smart enough to reach out and get help. We don't know the impact we have on others. We may think our words or actions don't matter, but they can truly be the difference between life and death for another. Saul had his priorities wrong, and it cost many people their lives or their freedom. When we, as Christians, get it wrong, it can cost someone's eternity.

What priorities do you need to change in order to live a Christ-centered life?

---

[47] Revelation 2:4.

We get to see how ugly Saul was, how deep into sin he was, and how God redeemed him. God forgave him for murdering and imprisoning God's children and used him in the most incredible way. Saul got to add numbers to God's family by bringing people to Christ in a great reversal of destiny. God took his sins and flipped them so they became the cornerstone of his ministry.

Has there been anything ugly in your past that God used as part of your ministry or testimony?

God, you never cease to amaze. Your grace is astonishing! You can take sinners like Saul, sinners like us, and mold us into Your image, using us to bring You glory and further Your kingdom. It blows me away. You are the reason we live. Thank You for Your unending mercy and grace. I pray You speak that message of mercy and grace into Your servant today. Remind us that we cannot out-sin Your grace. How we love You, Lord. Amen.

Week 6: Day 2

Good day to you, beloved! I hope that God refreshed your heart and renewed your spirit yesterday with the picture of grace Luke painted for us through the words of Acts 8. Today we are going to revisit Simon. Before I get too excited and spoil all of next week's material, please take a quick look at the story of Simon one more time (vv. 9–25). I know I said I wouldn't go into much detail about it, but this question keeps running through my mind. We have to look at it.

After reading Simon's story about his belief and baptism in verse 13 and Peter's rebuke in verses 20–24, do you think Simon was saved? Why or why not?

From the evidence in this passage and the rest of what we have learned so far in Acts, what do you think it takes to be saved?

I'm not going to share my thoughts on those subjects right now! You get to do that during discussion next week. I am certain it will be a very interesting and lively discussion. Please continue reading the rest of Acts 8:26–40. We are actually going to cover this single scene over the course of a couple days. Since it is one scene, we must read the entirety of it to stay in context.

What a wonderfully bizarre sequence of events! During this week's commentary, we studied how God was pushing the limits of the apostles' understanding by bringing the Samaritans into his kingdom. The incredible amount of supernatural intervention places emphasis on this event as part of God's plan. This passage pushes the limit of the Jewish Christian's understanding a little bit further with a hint of foreshadowing.[48]

Philip brings witness to the Samaritans, and an angel directs him to go down the southern road to Gaza and join an Ethiopian eunuch in his chariot. Do you remember when we studied the lame man in our third week of study? The Ethiopian eunuch would have been lumped together with him as an unworthy outcast. The eunuch wasn't even Jewish! As a eunuch, he was probably not a Jewish proselyte (convert); most likely, he was what theologians like to call a "God-fearer:" someone who would never be Jewish, but who believed God to be the One, True God and tried to live righteously as God has commanded. Though he is outside the Jewish Law and a Gentile, we find him reading and trying to understand Isaiah 53:7–8.

Why do you think God chose this specific man to be the first true Gentile to receive the gospel?

I keep picturing this scene. Luke tells us in verse 26 that the place where Philip was sent was a desert place, yet this Ethiopian eunuch was trying to understand the words of the prophet Isaiah on the side of the road. Instead of waiting to get where he was going to read and figure out the words of the prophet Isaiah, he parked on the side of the road in the middle of a desert. What are the first three words that come to your mind when you think of the desert?

1.

2.

---

[48] God has taken Philip out into the middle of the desert so he could find and witness to an Ethiopian eunuch. God is preparing the early Christians and the reader for the mission to the Gentiles with this small taste of foreshadowing, and he very purposefully brings in a Gentile—and a maimed one, at that.

3.

I think of *dusty, miserable,* and *my stupidly pale skin frying like southern-fried chicken.* These are not the most comfortable circumstances for reading the scriptures on the side of the road. I can't help but think that this man had a fierce desire to know God. Just like the lame man, this man was forced into a life that he most likely did not want. Can you imagine someone offering to become a eunuch? He could not have a wife or family, and was relegated to a life of servitude to the queen. Somehow, during his servitude to a pagan queen he had heard of this God of Abraham and had such a hunger to find Him that he was trying to decipher prophecies of Isaiah in the desert.

Has God ever brought you to a person that you thought was quite random—only to find out that he or she is hungry or searching for Him? What did you do?

In the few experiences I have had like this, I was there to discuss and give testimony about God's love and faithfulness. Mostly, I have not had the opportunity to see the seeds grow. But praise His Holy Name that it is not my job to water the seeds. It is only my job to plant them. Thank God that He is responsible for the rest! There was lots of talk last week about praying for our unbelieving family and friends, but be encouraged and have hope. You are not responsible for watering those seeds! The Spirit calls and whispers that invitation (Rev. 22:17). You are only responsible for dropping the seeds. God prepares the heart in His good time and purpose. Amen.

Also of notable importance is the fact that the eunuch was from Ethiopia. In Luke's time, the court of Queen Candace, whom verse 27 tells that the man served, was located in today's Sudan. During that time, Ethiopia was considered to be the ends of the earth. Therefore, Philip witnessing to the Ethiopian man was the literal fulfillment of Jesus's words in Acts 1:8 to take the gospel to the "ends of the earth."

Isn't it beautiful that God begins His mission to the Gentiles with the literal fulfilment of Jesus's directive? And so, the Gentile journey towards the gospel begins. I love that we get to walk this journey with them. Amen.

I rejoice to be with you today, studying God's incredible gift of His Word breathed onto the pages of our Bibles. The Jews believe that not only is every word of the Bible inspired, but so is every single letter—at least in the original language. What a gift that God has given us, to be able to read and study God's living Word, written by God through human hands. I praise His holy name!

No matter how much Bible we read, there is nothing like time spent reveling in the presence of our Savior. With that, please start your study today by rereading the scene with Philip and the Ethiopian eunuch (Acts 9:26–40) and then focus your mind on verses 30–35. I love the dialogue between the two men. I can just hear Philip asking, "Do you really know what you're reading?" The Ethiopian would say, "Uh, no."

Have there been any portions of scripture that you have read with absolutely no comprehension?

Did you come to understanding at some point? If so, how? If not, write it down so you can discuss it with your group.

I know I have! Even apart from Revelation, there have been quite a few times where I had to dig for a commentary, especially in the prophetic books or in some of the passages where Paul seems to contradict himself (which we know to be false). We have Bible studies with discussion so we can all help each other find understanding according to what God has revealed to you personally.

The incredible thing about scripture is that there is always a contextual meaning, but there is also always an application to your life. Hebrews 4:12 says, "For the word of God is living and active, sharper than any two-edged sword, piercing to the division of soul and of spirit, of joints and of marrow, and discerning the thoughts and intentions of the heart."

God's Word is alive and active. It pierces the soul and spirit, and it discerns the thoughts and intentions of the heart. That is why we can read the same verse a hundred times over and learn something new every time. It is inexplicable, but it is alive with the breath of God! That is why it is so important to be in the Word on a daily basis; it makes no rational sense, but the power of God's Word is unparalleled.

How has being in God's Word changed your life?

I think of heartbreak. Each time my heart feels like it is being ripped out of my chest, I cling to the Bible, knowing that it will bind it back together. Romans 5:3–5 tells us to rejoice in our sufferings because of character building that occurs while we are in it, but I think it is also because we are closest to God during those times.

In the Sermon on the Mount Jesus says, "Blessed are those who mourn, for they will be comforted."[49] In my life, those words from Jesus have proven so very true. During those times, I feel God's presence wrap around me so tightly. My very survival has depended upon His Word. I also think of all the transformation that has occurred because of my times of brokenness.

Have you gone through a period of brokenness where God's Word was essential to getting through it?

---

[49] Matthew 5:4.

As we turn back to Acts 8, please look at the scripture the Ethiopian was studying in verses 32–33. It is of no coincidence that he is reading Isaiah 53. Please turn there now and read this chapter of Isaiah in its entirety.

Please quickly summarize the idea of Isaiah 53:

Why do you think God directed this man to this specific passage?

I love God's Word. I love that the God we serve is the same today as He was thousands of years ago. His plan from thousands of years ago is the same as it is today. God directed the Ethiopian eunuch to this portion of scripture because He was preparing him to hear the message of Christ.

This passage speaks of salvation and redemption through Jesus's sacrifice, and it speaks of what Jesus came to do within His followers. We looked at this portion of Isaiah in our own studies in the first week because it prepared us to remember all the things God has done for us through His Son.

What do you think the eunuch's life was like?

Can you imagine the pain and humiliation he suffered and all the joys he had missed out on in life? This man was stripped of his very identity as a man: the inability to marry, to love a woman, to create children, to have a family of his own, and have a life of his own choosing. I cannot fathom his suffering, yet God directs him to this passage that speaks of the one who came to bear our grief, carry our sorrows, take our shame, and replace them with peace.

This man was searching for God and was in need of peace that only God could give. However, "the secret of seeking is not in our human ascent to God, but in God's descent to us."[50] God, in His grace and utmost mercy, descended to the eunuch through His disciple, Philip, who showed him the way to the God found in Isaiah 53. Philip showed the eunuch where he could find relief and live in joy and peace with the lot he was given. Isn't our God so good? Doesn't He simply blow you away with His grace and mercy? What kind of God reaches to the lowest just to show them they are loved and raise them up with His Son? Amen!

Do you have a testimony about God's descent to you in your time of need?

In addition to the spiritual blessings given by Christ, this portion of Isaiah speaks of a promise to the Gentiles of full participation of the "biblical religion in the future as a full member of God's people."[51] It speaks to those who are excluded and those who do not receive justice because of things outside of their control. It is possible that Luke sees this event between Philip and the Ethiopian as fulfillment of this particular prophecy out of Isaiah 53, which is why it is included verbatim within the text.[52]

This is the crack of the door guarding the wall between the Jews and the Gentiles. It is the first step toward welcoming the world into the fold of God's chosen people. Today, we can see the fulfillment of Jesus's sacrifice that welcomed the entire world. God has given us this picture of the very first ones to be invited.

God is truly impartial. There is no race, skin color, ethnicity, gender, label, or stereotype that stands between you and your Savior. Do not let any world-given label deter you from taking the God-given gift of Jesus.

---

[50] Guinness, The Call, 14.

[51] Ben Witherington III, The Acts of the Apostles: A Socio-Rhetorical Commentary, 296.

[52] Ibid.

As we continue through the Philip and the Ethiopian Eunuch narrative, I am once again reminded of God's miraculous provision. Following God can be so scary sometimes, but when we step out in faith into places we know God must actively work for us, we get to see Him do incredible things. As we finish this narrative today, I pray that you are reminded of the blessings and wonderful opportunities found in the scary places into which we are often called. Please skim the narrative found in Acts 8:26–40 to remind yourself of the context. I know it is a lot of rereading this week, but we have so much to learn from this episode of early church history. Let's dig in to verses 36–40.

God gave Philip an opening to share the gospel with the Ethiopian eunuch, and Philip was quick to seize it.

Has there ever been a time in your life when God asked you to share your testimony or a few words of the gospel with someone?

As we return to the scene out of Acts, we again read that Philip and the Ethiopian just happened upon some water in the middle of the desert. Some commentators believe that it was a miraculous occurrence—a God-given pool for this particular purpose of baptism. It wouldn't surprise me if it was because God is God—and He is pretty awesome.

Has God ever miraculously provided for you? Please don't be shy. Brag about your God!

Miracles of provision have happened on so many of the mission trips I have had the opportunity to attend. One specific miracle that comes to mind was with a group in Costa Rica. A man in our group had carved some wooden crosses and strung them as necklaces, but he only was able to make twenty-five of them. He felt led to give them out throughout the week, and somehow they never ran out. He had to have given out necklaces to more than a hundred people, but his twenty-five necklaces never ran out. He put in the effort to share his gifts, and God blessed his efforts so they were enough. God knew the men and women of these poor villages of Costa Rica needed a tangible reminder that God had not forgotten them, and He certainly provided. Praise God that He is still working today! How I wish I could hear your stories of God's provision!

As much as I love a good miracle testimony, there really is no indication in the text that this is the case in Acts 8—and we cannot be certain where the water came from. What we do know is that they came upon some water in the desert at just the right time, and the Ethiopian man did not hesitate to ask to be baptized.

God provides us with opportunities to grow in relationship with Him—be it through baptism, quiet whispers, or a simple longing of our spirits to be with Him. When was the last time God provided an opportunity of spiritual growth and you did not hesitate to take it?

What happened because you took that opportunity?

Isn't it simply amazing that God desires a relationship so much that He calls to us and puts people, places, opportunities in our paths that lead us straight to Him? God gave the eunuch such an opportunity and he did not hesitate for one second. We read of his baptism in verse 38, but verse 39 is bizarre! Right after they come up out of the water, Philip is simply picked up from the desert and whisked away to Azotus (about 30-50 miles north/northwest depending on where Philip encountered the Ethiopian man on the road from Jerusalem to Gaza). Philip continues his journey as if nothing incredible has happened and just keeps on walking and preaching until he reached Caesarea. If God wanted to just whisk me away somewhere, I am totally down! It's like *Star Trek* of the first century. The funnier thing is that the Ethiopian man doesn't even stop to question Philip's sudden disappearance. He just goes on his way, singing the good Lord's praises. Oh that we would have such faith!

This, my friends, forces us to look at ourselves and examine our own faith. Sit for a moment with God and ask Him to show you any unbelief or lack of faith you may have.

Is there any unbelief with which you are struggling today?

Write a prayer here that He may grow your faith:

The incredible thing about God is that He wills us to have faith in abundance. Over and over and over, we are told that faith is credited as righteousness[53] and that when we ask for things from God, it must be done in faith with no doubting.[54] Matthew 21:22 tells us that anything we ask for that is in the will of God will be given to us if we ask in faith—even when we ask for faith itself! God wills us to have faith in Him. We know He desires us to have faith in Him; therefore, when we ask for more faith, it is by His Word that He says we will receive it. Believe!

---

[53] Romans 4:3.
[54] James 1:6.

Week 6: Day 5

We are taking a brief field trip from Acts today. Remaining with our theme of faith that we began yesterday, we are going to look at Abraham and Jacob and the faith that has become the standard for Jews and Christians alike.

Pop quiz! What nationality were the early Christ-followers found in Acts 1-10?

Jewish! The father of their nation held the gold-standard for faith. And what a faith it was! The ancient word for the kind of faith Abraham had is "chutzpah." Today, this word has almost a negative connotation, meaning particularly audacious or without thought of social standard, bordering on impudence. Originally, however, chutzpah described a faith with utter *tenacity*; it was a faith that clung to God's promises, demanding fulfillment. Please find Genesis 18 and read verses 22-33.

God tells Abraham the He is about to destroy Sodom. How many times did Abraham ask God for mercy?

Chutzpah is the kind of faith that gives Abraham the guts to remind God that He is a righteous and merciful God: a God who wouldn't kill the righteous along with the wicked. Can you imagine? What faith!

Have you ever had the *chutzpah* to remind God of His character and ask Him for mercy or blessing? What happened?

Please turn the pages of your Bible a little further and read Genesis 32:22-27. Summarize this scene:

Jacob is wrestling with a man all night. Some scholars believe this is an angel, and yet some also believe this is a preincarnate appearance of Jesus due to Jacob's words in Genesis 32:30. Jacob refuses to let the man win.

What does he say in response to the man's request in verse 26?

Oh how I love those words: "I will not let you go unless you bless me." This phrase wraps up the idea of chutzpah in a nutshell. Beginning with the patriarchs of Judaism, the Jewish culture clings to God's promises with a tenacity bordering on insubordination. They remind God of His promises and demand fulfillment with chutzpah. Our western culture typically discourages this kind of tenacity by replacing "I will not let go unless you bless me," with "Thy will be done," and giving up without fighting for the blessing. Don't get me wrong, we must absolutely walk in God's will and we will not bear fruit unless we are walking in His will. However, chutzpah is based on demanding fulfillment of the things God has already promised.

What are some of the biblical things God has promised us?

Is there anything specific God has promised you: a vision of the future, a goal, a ministry, etc.?

God promises to work every situation for the good of us who love Him, according to His good purpose (Romans 8:28). Do you believe that? Do you hold Him to His promise and refuse to lose faith in Him, clinging to the promise until the moment of fulfillment? God promises in Matthew 11:28-29 to ease our burdens by taking them upon Himself. Do you believe that? Do you cling to Him in desperation until He gives you peace and rest? God promises in Isaiah 40:29-31 to give strength to the weary, to give power to the weak, to give endurance to the frail. *Do you believe him?* If God has made a promise—in His written Word, or through His still, small whisper into your soul—remind Him of His promise. Cling to it with *chutzpah,* holding firm with the words of Jacob, "I will *not* let you go until you bless me!"

In the Old Testament, God repeatedly blesses those who cling to His promises with chutzpah. If God has promised you something, beloved, you better hold on long enough to receive the blessing.

What did God speak to you this week?

God, how I bless Your name! I believe You desire to grow our faith through proving Yourself faithful. Help us learn to be patient in waiting upon You—help us see that Your timing is truly perfect. We bless You, Father. Thank You for Your faithfulness. Amen!

WEEK 7
Commentary: The Miracle of Grace

Do you remember your conversion? Do you remember when you finally gave in to God's call and faced the sin in your life and turned it over to Him? I was raised in the church, so I gave God my life in fifth-grade confirmation class. I was baptized in my preacher's pool.

It wasn't long after that, however, that I lost my way. I became very rebellious and followed my own path for a long time. Looking back, I never lost belief in God's existence. I just didn't want Him running my life. He continued after me, though, and He kept calling me back. It took my life falling apart because of the consequences of my choices before I finally returned to Him—but once I did, I returned with fervor. I had tasted life without God, and it was not a life I wanted. It wasn't a life I wanted for others either. I was hungry for the Word, and I was hungry to share my God with others. Some people let God into their life easy, accepting Him and His direction with joy and peace. As we will see today, others—like Saul and me—need to learn the hard way.

Please open your Bible with me to Acts 9:1–9:

> [1] But Saul, still breathing threats and murder against the disciples of the Lord, went to the high priest [2] and asked him for letters to the synagogues at Damascus, so that if he found any belonging to the Way, men or women, he might bring them bound to Jerusalem. [3] Now as he went on his way, he approached Damascus, and suddenly a light from heaven shone around him. [4] And falling to

the ground he heard a voice saying to him, "Saul, Saul, why are you persecuting me?" ⁵ And he said, "Who are you, Lord?" And he said, "I am Jesus, whom you are persecuting. ⁶ But rise and enter the city, and you will be told what you are to do." ⁷ The men who were traveling with him stood speechless, hearing the voice but seeing no one. ⁸ Saul rose from the ground, and although his eyes were opened, he saw nothing. So they led him by the hand and brought him into Damascus. ⁹ And for three days he was without sight, and neither ate nor drank.

The Saul we see in the beginning of Acts 9 is no different than the one we saw in chapter 7 or the beginning of chapter 8. He is "breathing threats and murder" against the disciples of Christ. He was only given permission (probably by Caiaphas, the high priest) to bind men and women belonging to the Way (what early Christians called themselves) and bring them back to Jerusalem. He was not given permission to execute anyone. He may have wished death on these men and women, but he was only able to imprison them. Saul was a self-professed zealot. In Jesus day, the Jewish zealots were a small sect of Pharisees who used violence to cleanse Israel in order to bring about the coming of the Messiah. What he believed in, he believed with an obsessive passion and acted accordingly. We see from these first glimpses of Saul a serious desire for the restoration of Israel, which he is willing to live out through action—even if that action included violence.

However, as Saul is on his way to purify Damascus of the "blasphemous" sect of Christ-followers, something incredible happens: he has an encounter with the risen Christ.

Jesus says, "Saul, Saul, why are you persecuting me?"

Can you hear the hurt in these words?

Jesus indicates that He is so closely bound to His followers that when Saul persecutes any of Christ's disciples, he is persecuting Christ directly. God feels it when any of His children are hurt or persecuted. We see God associating Himself with our pain many times throughout the Bible. In Revelation 6, there is the blood of the martyrs on the altar in front of God's throne, and the blood continually cries out for vengeance. God doesn't forget. He remembers every single one who gave their blood in His name, and He physically and emotionally goes through every second of it with them—even after death—until He dispenses His righteous judgment.

Psalm 58:6 says, "You have kept count of my tossings; put my tears in your bottle. Are they not in your book?"

God keeps count of every tear shed, and He feels them too. He feels each time we hurt ourselves through bad choices, blatant sin, or inadvertent mistakes. We have the ability to hurt God because He chooses to bind Himself so closely to us that He feels everything we feel. Like Jesus said, Saul was not just persecuting God's children—he was persecuting God. Saul was not just hurting God's children—he was hurting God.

After Jesus states his charge against him, Saul wants to know who this person is and addresses him as "Lord." Most likely, this word means that Saul knew he was addressing a supernatural being, but he did not understand who it was. Maybe he thought it was an angel of God. He did not know he was addressing the risen Christ.

Jesus tells Saul to continue into Damascus and wait until someone tells him what to do. I love the description of the men who were accompanying Saul; they stood speechless. In the presence of God, I think I would be struck speechless too. Verse 7 tells us that they heard the voice, but they saw no one. This experience was for Saul alone.

In Acts 22:9, during a repetition of Saul's conversion story, Saul (who was renamed "Paul") tells us that the men did not hear the message. They heard the voice, but they did not hear words nor were they able to comprehend the message. In this personal encounter, God made sure Saul alone got the message.

We serve a personal, intimate God who speaks directly to each one of us. When God speaks to you, He is giving you a message meant for you and you alone. God doesn't give "blanket statements." He is way too intimate for that. He whispers in your ear like the most tender of lovers, speaking words that lift your soul, fill you with peace, and give hope for your future.

Before we move on in this chapter, I want to point out a couple things. Witherington says,

> Without question the story of Saul's "conversion" is one of the most important events, if not the most important event, that Luke records in acts. The importance is shown by the fact that Luke tells the story no less than 3 full times, from 3 slightly different angles, with the later narratives in Acts 22 and 26 supplementing the basic third-person account in Acts 9.[55]

This narrative account is one of the most important events in Acts. We talked about Luke only having a short amount of space to write thirty years of material; therefore, only the most important events received a lot of detail. The fact that Luke repeats this story twice more means that he thought it to be of the utmost importance.

Most likely, Luke repeated Paul's conversion story due to the scope of Paul's mission. Conversely, the apostles' mission was to the Jews and to prayer. They were the cornerstone of the church and set up systems to ensure that the gospel message stayed true to Jesus's words. While their job was obviously vital to the early church, Paul was a missionary of epic proportions. After Acts 13, much of the rest of Acts is dedicated to Paul's ministry, some for which Luke was actually present (according to his writings). Luke saw Paul's ministry as one of utmost importance, and the beginnings of it bore repetition.

Let's turn to the rest of Saul's conversion story in verses 10–19:

> [10] Now there was a disciple at Damascus named Ananias. The Lord said to him in a vision, "Ananias." And he said, "Here I am, Lord." [11] And the Lord said to him, "Rise and go to the street called Straight, and at the house of Judas look for a man of Tarsus named Saul, for behold, he is praying, [12] and he has seen in a vision a man named Ananias come in and lay his hands on him so that he might regain his sight." [13] But Ananias answered, "Lord, I have heard from many about this man, how much evil he has done to your saints at Jerusalem. [14] And here he

---

[55] Witherington, *The Acts of the Apostles: A Socio-Rhetorical Commentary*, 303.

has authority from the chief priests to bind all who call on your name." [15] But the Lord said to him, "Go, for he is a chosen instrument of mine to carry my name before the Gentiles and kings and the children of Israel. [16] For I will show him how much he must suffer for the sake of my name." [17] So Ananias departed and entered the house. And laying his hands on him he said, "Brother Saul, the Lord Jesus who appeared to you on the road by which you came has sent me so that you may regain your sight and be filled with the Holy Spirit." [18] And immediately something like scales fell from his eyes, and he regained his sight. Then he rose and was baptized; [19] and taking food, he was strengthened.

This passage is full of God's direct action and interaction, which tells us that He found this conversion to be of utmost importance to the fulfillment of His plan. Jesus personally confronted Saul and blinded him so he would have to wait upon another to give him instruction. On the other hand, God sent a vision to Ananias, and they just hung out and had a conversation.

Did you notice the difference between Ananias and Saul's responses when spoken to by the Lord? Ananias knew immediately who was talking to him, and he responded much like an Old Testament prophet. He said, "Here I am, Lord." This is a whole lesson in of itself. When God speaks to you, do you know His voice? Do you listen and respond with an open heart and a willing mind?

Jesus called Ananias, and he was ready to hear the Lord's message. Jesus tells him to go to Judas's house on Straight Street and look for a man from Tarsus named Saul (the first time Luke mentions Saul's place of birth). He will find Saul praying there because Saul received a vision that Ananias was coming to lay hands on him. This verse indicates a double vision: Jesus is speaking to Ananias in a vision, and at the same time, Saul is receiving a vision about Ananias. This little tidbit shows God's omnipresence.

Ananias replies out of his fear from what he has heard about Saul— about the evil Saul has committed against Jesus's disciples. His reply indicates that he has heard about the decree that Saul is able to bind followers of the Way and take them off to Jerusalem.

Ananias knew of Saul, but he had to trust God that Saul would not kill or imprison him. We, the church, can be like Ananias. Sometimes God calls us to lavish His love, grace, and mercy on one who seems to be dangerous or evil. We don't understand or like it, we are scared by it, or we are angry. When our judgment clouds our vision of God's plan, we refuse to extend the same grace that we have been given.

What if Ananias had said no? Where would the church be today if there was not a specific missionary dedicated to taking the gospels to the Gentiles? Peter wavered many times about God's message that the gospel was for the Gentiles.[56] I doubt he would have fulfilled that role. As I pondered this lesson, I kept being reminded of the sinful woman who anointed Jesus's feet with her perfume and the men who were angry that she was even in Jesus's presence.

Turn with me to Luke 7:36–50:

> [36] One of the Pharisees asked Jesus to have dinner with him, so Jesus went to his home and sat down to eat. [37] When a certain immoral woman from that city heard he was eating there, she brought a beautiful alabaster jar filled with expensive perfume. [38] Then she knelt behind him at his feet, weeping. Her tears fell on his feet, and she wiped them off with her hair. Then she kept kissing his feet and putting perfume on them.
>
> [39] When the Pharisee who had invited him saw this, he said to himself, "If this man were a prophet, he would know what kind of woman is touching him. She's a sinner!"
>
> [40] Then Jesus answered his thoughts. "Simon," he said to the Pharisee, "I have something to say to you."
>
> "Go ahead, Teacher," Simon replied.
>
> [41] Then Jesus told him this story: "A man loaned money to two people—500 pieces of silver[i] to one and

---

[56] Galatians 2:11–13.

50 pieces to the other. ⁴²But neither of them could repay him, so he kindly forgave them both, canceling their debts. Who do you suppose loved him more after that?"

⁴³Simon answered, "I suppose the one for whom he canceled the larger debt."

"That's right," Jesus said. ⁴⁴Then he turned to the woman and said to Simon, "Look at this woman kneeling here. When I entered your home, you didn't offer me water to wash the dust from my feet, but she has washed them with her tears and wiped them with her hair. ⁴⁵You didn't greet me with a kiss, but from the time I first came in, she has not stopped kissing my feet. ⁴⁶You neglected the courtesy of olive oil to anoint my head, but she has anointed my feet with rare perfume.

⁴⁷"I tell you, her sins—and they are many—have been forgiven, so she has shown me much love. But a person who is forgiven little shows only little love." ⁴⁸Then Jesus said to the woman, "Your sins are forgiven."

⁴⁹The men at the table said among themselves, "Who is this man, that he goes around forgiving sins?"

⁵⁰And Jesus said to the woman, "Your faith has saved you; go in peace."

The men doubted Jesus was a prophet simply because He allowed her into His presence. In verse 47, Jesus says, "Therefore I tell you, her sins, which are many are forgiven—for she loved much. But he who is forgiven little, loves little."

We have no idea what other's lives have been like. We don't know the circumstances or understand the experiences that led to who they are today. Who are we to withhold mercy and grace? I urge music-loving folks to listen to "Alabaster Box" by CeCe Winans. If you don't care for gospel music, I hope you at least look up the lyrics.

The whole point of this song is that we don't know the cost of another's sins. The song speaks of all the riches that the woman had received and the incredible personal cost incurred upon earning them. She was not simply pouring her perfume on Jesus's feet—she was giving Him her sins, her guilt, and her shame. Her sin was what bought the perfume, and where else do you lay your sin but at the feet of Jesus? We don't know what led others into sin, but there is an incredible, loving, merciful God in heaven who does. We leave our sins at His feet, and we lead others who are in need of His grace to His feet.

What if Ananias had said no? I think that God would have used someone else to free Saul of his blindness. Thankfully, Ananias had enough trust and love in God that he followed God's direction and had mercy on Saul. When he goes to Saul, Saul has been fasting in silence for three days (v. 9). I wonder what Saul was thinking of during those three days. I wonder if he was looking into his alabaster box and pouring his tears on Jesus feet. I wonder if God gave Saul all this time to see the depth of his sin and see the depth of his need. I sent you to that song because I want you to see what happens when someone sees the depth of his or her need for God. It produces a fire and a zeal for Christ. Saul was always full of zeal and passion for what he believed in. After Jesus confronted him in his sin, Saul's zeal becomes founded in love instead of law and judgment.

Let's read this last little section of verses 19b–22:

> For some days he was with the disciples at Damascus. [20] And immediately he proclaimed Jesus in the synagogues, saying, "He is the Son of God." [21] And all who heard him were amazed and said, "Is not this the man who made havoc in Jerusalem of those who called upon this name? And has he not come here for this purpose, to bring them bound before the chief priests?" [22] But Saul increased all the more in strength, and confounded the Jews who lived in Damascus by proving that Jesus was the Christ.

"This was a radical change of religious direction, and it was accompanied by a radical change of action: the active persecutor became an even more active preacher and evangelist."[57] Saul experienced a radical change—beginning from the core of his beliefs, stemming out to every word he utters and every action he takes.

---

[57] Barrett, *Acts,* 442.

It is so easy to use grace as an excuse to sin casually, knowing that grace will eventually erase it. We are wrong when we think like that. Grace is the exact opposite: Grace is a call to action! Romans 12:6 says, "Having gifts that differ according to the grace given to us, let us use them!" There is a direct correlation between how much you grow toward God and how much love you pour on those around you. You can't help it. The more you love God, the more you see people through God's eyes and love them. Just like Jesus told Peter in John 21:15, "If you love me, feed my lambs!"

We are forgiven because of God's incredible love for us, but it doesn't stop there. Matthew 10:8 says, "Freely you have received; freely give!" Because we have freely received the gift of grace, we have a responsibility to freely give grace to others and lead them to the throne from where true grace flows. No matter what, we cannot be tempted into hoarding God's grace for ourselves.

As we read in the last little section, Saul took his call to action very seriously. God gave him three days to take in God's grace—to fully receive it, to believe it, to be humbled by it—and Saul turned around and immediately takes on the mantel of a disciple of Christ and a missionary to the Gentile world.

Oh, that we would be the same. Lord, I pray that we will open our eyes to Your grace, accept the grace You have extended us, see it as a call to action, and extend it to others. I pray that we will see the depths of the pit from where You pulled us and rejoice and love You all the more for it. In Your precious and holy name, Amen!

Week 7: Day 1

Hello, dear one. It is with a bittersweet heart that I write this commentary and discussion guide today because it will be our last week together in homework. What a journey this has been! I cannot tell you how appreciative I am that you chose to do this study with me. And more than that—you stayed! You have persevered through the past seven weeks—sometimes with tears and sometimes with joy. I thank God for you and your desire to learn about Him and His Word.

Today is quite a day for learning. As you turn to God now, I hope you will ask for Him to bestow the brainpower it takes to absorb all the little facts and tidbits that make Saul's story come alive to us who live in such a very different time. We ask Him to guide you in today's reading and give you a fresh word and a new understanding.

Please open your Bibles and read Acts 9:1–19.

We went over this material during our last session, but I want to point out a couple of things. You may have heard me mention that Luke retold Saul's conversions story two more times within Acts (Acts 22:1–16 and 26:12–18). Saul's conversion stories are told by two different people to three different audiences; please list the speaker and audience of each passage:

Acts 9:1–19:

Acts 22:1–16:

Acts 26:12–18:

The first account is told by Luke to you. He is telling the reader the account in the third person, but the next two are first-person accounts told by Saul (his name had already changed to Paul). The scene out of Acts 22 is a little chaotic, but I will give you a short summary to clear it up.

This is Paul's last time in Jerusalem as he makes his way to Rome. In Acts 21, Paul visits James in Jerusalem and purifies himself to enter the temple. In 21:27, the Jews from Asia stirred up the crowd, seized Paul, dragged him to the temple court, and beat him with intent to kill.

The Roman military tribune was in charge of the cohort. The commander, Claudius Lysias (as told in Acts 23:26), heard about it and rescued Paul with up to a thousand men. He immediately arrests Paul, binds him in chains between two soldiers, and hauls him off to prison.

Paul tells them that he is a Roman citizen and asks to address the crowd. He is given permission, and thus begins his miraculous story of conversion. Paul speaks to the Jews in their Hebrew language while he is in Roman custody, appealing to their sense of ethnic brotherhood one last time. The Jews do not accept him, nor do they accept his testimony and instead call for his death. While in custody, Paul uses his Roman citizenship to save his life and demand a trial by Caesar. His wishes are granted and he remains in Roman custody for the rest of his life, as he journeys his way to Rome to appear before Caesar.

In chapter 26, we see another stop on this journey to Rome. For two years, Paul has been in custody at Caesarea, the seat of Rome in Greece (first under Governor Felix and then under Festus). Chapter 25 introduces King Agrippa and his wife, Bernice; this is Herod Agrippa II (AD 27–100), the king of Chalcis (a small kingdom north and east of Judea).[58] Paul gives his third and last testimony of conversion to them.

In response, Agrippa declares Paul's innocence and says, "This man could have been set free if he had not appealed to Caesar."[59]

Paul knew very clearly that if he followed God's plan straight into the Roman Empire,[60] he would die there.

---

[58] Witherington, *The Acts of the Apostles: A Socio-Rhetorical Commentary*, 727.
[59] Acts 26:32.
[60] Acts 21:1–14.

Has God ever asked anything of you, and you knew it was going to be fraught with peril (emotional or physical)?

Is your love for God bigger than anything else you hold dear, including your own life? What about your family's lives?

If you have been following the trend of Christian persecution in the middle east, you know that being a Christian there is a question of life or death. I read a story not too long ago where a man was forced to watch Islamic terrorists torture his son by cutting off his fingers, rather than disavow Jesus Christ. The terrorists ended up killing both he and his son. Yet another story I just read detailed the burning alive of Christian women because of their faith in Jesus. We do not yet have to make these decisions, but there may come a time when we do. If and when that time comes, will you be prepared and willing to lose your life, or your family's lives, in the name of Christ? God, how I pray that you will give us the courage to follow you even into death.

Luke tells us three times how Saul/Paul turned from his murderous, zealous ways to become a peace-loving Christ-follower. Each time Paul told his conversion story, he gave us a few different details dependent upon which he felt were the most pertinent in the immediate situation. For you scholars, I have provided a chart detailing these few minor differences should you be interested in comparing them.

Acts 9:1–9	Acts 22:1–16	Acts 26:12–18
Saul asks high priest for letters to the synagogues providing authorization to extradite Christians to Jerusalem (v. 1)	Saul received letters from the high priest and council to extradite Christians to Jerusalem for punishment (v. 5)	Saul received authorization from the chief priests (v. 10)
Light from heaven flashed about him (v. 3)	At noon, great light from heaven shone about me (v. 6)	Midday, light from heaven shining around me and those with me (v. 13)
Fell to ground, heard a voice (v. 4)	Same as Acts 9 (v. 7)	We all fell to ground, I heard a voice in Hebrew (v. 14)
"Saul, Saul why do you persecute me?"	Same as Acts 9	Same as Acts 9, with the added "It hurts you to kick against the goads."

I know today was filled with history and lots of different names and dates, and it may have been more than you bargained. What I hope you remember is that Saul chose to put God's will above his own—even unto death. I hope you are challenged and truly question whose will you choose to follow. Do you trust God to do what is best for you and your family in every single situation you face? Do you believe that He holds you in the palm of His hand and will provide for you in every situation? When your time comes, will you choose God over your will, even when it is hard, scary, or dangerous? Give us your courage, God, and the faith to hold true to You in the midst of any adversary. Amen.

Week 7: Day 2

Good day to you, beloved! It is indeed a good day because today is not nearly as full of facts and information as yesterday. Please skim chapter 9 of Acts if you need a little refresher as we drop back into the context of Saul's conversion. As always, spend some time with God before you start your lesson for today.

Last week, I mentioned what happened once Saul finally made it into Damascus and had to wait three days for Ananias. One thing I did not point out, however, is what Jesus told Ananias in the vision in verse 15–16.

Please write a summary of these two verses here:

God was so proactive about Saul's conversion because he had a lot riding on Saul! I love that Ananias found out about this before Saul did.

Why do you think God told Ananias about His plan for Saul?

It's possible that Ananias needed a bit more encouragement before he could get up the courage to face the "savage persecutor" named Saul. Did you catch what Jesus said he was showing Saul? "For I will show him how much he must suffer for the sake of my name" (v. 16). Can you imagine knowing the trials you will have to endure when faced with making a lifelong choice?

Can you imagine going into a marriage, knowing exactly what challenges your marriage will face: maybe a rebellious child, maybe alcoholism, maybe an affair, maybe just a slow growing apart that rends the heart to pieces. Do you think you would have the courage to make the choice to stay? That is exactly what Saul had to face. He was, for all intents and purposes, married to God. God was his life partner through everything—through sickness and health, through persecution and times of community, through freedom and bondage—it was just Saul and God. Saul had a couple different partners who would travel with him, including Luke, but ultimately he was with God. God showed him *everything* he would have to suffer if he made the choice to take up the mantel of a disciple of Christ. Saul knew that if he chose Christ, he would ultimately give his life for Him. Saul still chose to say yes.

I wonder if God showed Saul the depth of his sin during these three days; then, while he was staring his need and depravity in the face, gave him the option of eternal life that will include suffering on this planet, or a mortal life devoid of suffering, but also devoid of eternity spent in God's presence.

I keep going back to what happened during these three days!

Why do you think God gave Saul three days in his blindness before Ananias arrived?

I don't know the answer. I do know that we are tested in the waiting. We *learn* in the waiting. We learn about God, and we learn about ourselves.

Have you ever been in a time of waiting? If so, what did you learn from it?

My times of waiting have taught me that God was *preparing* me for whatever came next. If He wasn't preparing me, He was preparing the other person or preparing the situation. I don't know if God works like this all the time—or only with me because He knows I am so impulsive—but it seems like I wait ... and wait ... and wait ... and then wait some more.

When God finally says, "Go," I am off to the races!

Once the waiting time is over, the time for action is immediate, and it all falls into place because He has done all the prep work. If you are in a time of waiting, continue with endurance and patience. Know that He is preparing you, another, or the situation. When the time comes, you can go without fear or anxiety because He has already set you up for victory!

Week 7: Day 3

I loved our lesson yesterday. The three days Saul spent fasting before God pull at my heart and pique my imagination. I hope it meant as much to you as it did to me. We have an exciting day before us in the Word. Go before God humbly and ask for His grace and wisdom to pour into you today.

Please continue our reading for this week by reading Acts 9:19–25.

Once Ananias came, Saul wasted no time in getting baptized and then getting to work. He stayed with the disciples and immediately began teaching in the synagogues. It didn't take long before those confounded Jews plotted to kill Saul.

Isn't the thin line between love and hate funny? Saul the persecutor was a superhero among the Jews. He was the champion of their faith, purging the temples of the "blasphemous sect" that was spreading like wildfire. They loved him dearly.

Instead of bringing prisoners, Saul popped up in Damascus and spouted the same message as the disciples of the Way. He was teaching in the synagogue and talking about a "blasphemous" vision in which a resurrected Jesus appeared to him! It did not take long before the Jews were watching the gates day and night, waiting for the opportune time to kill him. God provided, and Saul heard of the plot. His followers took him to the wall at night and lowered him through a basket. He escaped and journeyed on to Jerusalem.

Have you ever been on the receiving end of a love that quickly turned to hatred?

Have you loved someone dearly until something happened and you began to "strongly dislike" him or her?

Strong emotions lead to other strong emotions. Only those we allow ourselves to love can hurt us enough to evoke such negative strong emotions. It is hard to forgive when the hurt is rooted deeply.

Are you holding on to something God is calling you to forgive? If you are holding on to hate or anger for someone you once loved, please write a prayer right now that God would help you release it.

As we continue on in Acts 9, we read of Saul's return to Jerusalem. It was the first time he would enter it as a Christ-follower. Please read Acts 9:26–31 to find out what happens.

In your opinion, why didn't the disciples believe Saul was a changed man?

I wonder if it was one time that the apostles' fear won out over God's quiet whisper. I might be assuming too much here, but I do wonder.

Do you think God would have given them a nudge that Saul was now His?

All but one was afraid and did not believe him—all but Barnabas. Barnabas means, "son of encouragement," and in this context, he was living out his name. He was the first to believe Saul, and he encouraged the others to do the same through a summary of Saul's conversion (v. 27).

Thanks to Barnabas's interference and encouragement, the apostles received Saul, and Saul continued to teach among the apostles and the Hellenists. The Jews heard Saul preaching the gospel of Christ and sought to kill him; once again, Saul was quickly shipped out of there. Verse 30 tells us that Saul's "brother" (in Christ) took him down to Caesarea and sent him off to Tarsus.

In this verse, Luke uses a literary technique that leaves off with Saul in the same place that he will be when Luke picks up his story again in Acts 11:25 (Tarsus). While Saul is traveling, Luke shifts his focus back to the growing Christian church.

What is happening within the church in verse 31?

Luke is giving Theophilus a small glimpse into the church as a whole at this particular moment. Growing in peace and walking in fear of the Lord and comfort of the Holy Spirit, it multiplied. It is a beautiful picture.

Luke gives us these small glimpses so we can remember that the church was so much bigger than the specific events that Luke spelled out in detail. While Saul was in Jerusalem, a mass of Christians was being built up into the body of Christ. Sometimes we get so caught up in the small things that we forget to appreciate the beauty of the fuller picture.

Is there anything in your life right now that keeps blocking your vision of the beauty of the bigger picture?

If so, give it to God and ask Him to allow your scope of vision to widen so that you can rest in the beauty of His picture.

I often become so distraught with the state of my community, my nation, and this world that I forget that God is still present and active within it. I see the non-existent morality portrayed in the media and forget that God is raising up a generation strong in Him, with a passion and a fire to love and serve Him that I find outrageous. I see the Christians in Africa, Asia and the middle east being imprisoned, tortured, and murdered for their faith and forget that God is using that persecution to spread His message like wildfire. We get so caught up in the negative that we forget to look for the way God is working in and through it. When you become overwhelmed because of the ugliness of the world, specifically look for the ways God is at work in those situations. What you find may blow you away! Thank you, God, for your incredible ways! Amen.

Good day to you, dearest one! I want to start today with the words from Psalm 33:1–3:

> Shout for joy in the Lord, O you righteous!
> Praise befits the upright.
> ² Give thanks to the Lord with the lyre;
> make melody to him with the harp of ten strings!
> ³ Sing to him a new song;
> play skillfully on the strings, with loud shouts.

As I ponder the blessing and gift of grace, which God lavishes upon us, I am led to simply rejoice in Him. I pray that God pours His eternal blessing of joy into your hearts that you may shout for joy, praising God, thanking Him and singing Him a new song.

That being said, please read Acts 9:32–35.

We now have pushed pause on the story of Saul and returned our focus to Peter. This portion of scriptures tells of Peter coming to a place called Lydda, which is one of the towns Philip ministered to as he made his way from Azotus to Caesarea (Acts 8:40). Again, Luke portrays Peter as one in a long line of healing prophets.

What happened in verses 32–35?

How gracious is our God who seeks out the least of the least? In this passage, Peter finds a paralyzed man and simply tells him to get up. The words in verse 34—"rise and make your bed"—indicate complete healing. If a man could get up and prepare for his day, he was considered healed. God doesn't do anything halfway. Amen? When He seeks us out to heal us, He heals us completely so we may continue on His path for our lives. As always, Luke gives us the miracle and the resultant belief of the witnesses.

Who does Luke say turned to the Lord because of Aeneas's healing?

All of them! "And all the residents of Lydda and Sharon" turned to the Lord (v. 35). Imagine if we could all have such belief and faith today! Each time God works in our lives, it is so we can give him praise and glory. He heals us because we are His, and He loves us so powerfully. He also asks that we love others enough to share our stories of God's work in our lives in order to bring others to Christ.

This week's miracle is the miracle of grace.

Have you shared your miracle of grace story with another?

Are you using the work God has done in your life to build up the kingdom of God?

Please pray that God will provide you with opportunities to share your grace story, the vision to see the opportunities, and the courage to seize the opportunity and share it with boldness.

The incredible thing we see happen in Acts over and over again is that God did not use these miracles to bring a few people into His family. He used them to bring massive amounts of people to Himself.

What do you think would happen if we believed and prayed for God to start a revival in our churches, our cities, our states, our nations, and our world?

Do you have the faith to believe that He can light this world on *fire* for Him? Do you believe that He hears the prayers of the righteous and is waiting on His perfect timing to begin a revolution in this world?

I pray today—and I hope you will join me in this prayer—for God to do a *mighty* work in this world and bring people to Himself in unprecedented numbers!

Today is our last day of homework together. I pray that God has blessed you beyond measure with your perseverance in His Word. I cannot thank you enough for your time and efforts, and I am praying for you and praising God for you.

Please finish this last day of study by completing your reading of Acts 9:36–43.

Who was Dorcas—and what did she do in her community?

Luke is very particular about the examples he gives so that he can promote impartiality in the kingdom of God. This example, combined with yesterday's example of Aeneas's healing shows that God was impartial to social status, gender, ethnicity, and anything else.

These last two passages in Acts 9:32–43 show us that Luke firmly believed that God loved and cared for everyone equally, and He used each and every available person to further the glory of His kingdom in whatever capacity they were able—man or woman, rich or poor, Jew or Gentile. Praise Him! God only sees us as the masterpiece He created—not by any of the divisive labels we force upon others.

Have there been any specific examples of God's impartiality that have struck you? Please share!

Luke calls Dorcas a "disciple," which indicates that she had status and importance within the community of believers in Joppa. Since she was described as a woman full of charity, she was most likely a woman of means. Luke points out her economic status specifically so Theophilus can relate to her. It has the added bonus of teaching us that money doesn't matter—except as far as we can help others with it. Luke provided so much more detail about Dorcas to specifically point out the work she was doing and highlight it as something specifically noteworthy for the early Christians.

What does verse 37 say happened to Dorcas?

The disciples were in mourning, but they were not without faith. They had heard that Peter was in Lydda and sent for him, asking him to make haste and come quickly. When Peter obliges and enters the room, widows were weeping and showing tunics. The tunics described are the tunics that the women wore under their cloaks, directly next to the skin. Dorcas made these garments for the widows, again highlighting the work she was doing among the needy.

What is the first thing Peter does in verse 40?

He puts them all outside. This is the part of Jesus's teachings where he says not to pray in public to gain attention.[61] Peter was already such a highly respected man, especially within the Jewish Christian community, and he did not want to steal God's glory in making it about himself. The woman was already dead when Peter was sent for. Therefore, he knew he was not there to simply heal her. He was there to ask God to raise her from the dead.

In John 11:43, Jesus raises Lazarus from the dead simply by telling Lazarus to arise and come out of the tomb. There are quite a few other

---

[61] Matthew 6:5.

instances when Jesus raises people from the dead simply by touching them or by telling them to arise. This is *not* the case with Peter.

What is the second thing Peter does in verse 40?

He got on his knees and prayed.

There is *power* when we are on our knees in front of our Creator. When we hit the floor in supplication to our Father in heaven, we are *unlimited* in what God can do through us. Amen!

When was the last time you asked something outrageous of God and believed that He would do it?

God blessed Peter's request and breathed sweet life back into her mortal body. When Dorcas arose, Peter presented her to all the saints and widows of Joppa.

What does Luke say happened in verse 42?

And many believed in the Lord. For Luke, miracles equaled conversions. There is only one reason God does a miracle, still to this day: that many may hear and believe. Your testimony matters, dear one!

What does Peter do according to verse 43?

We will look at this much more in the last commentary. We are in for a wild ride as we study chapter 10, the last chapter of our study. Suffice it to say that God was using these days staying with Simon the tanner to prepare Peter for the next phase of God's plan. God does *so much* in the waiting. Praise Him who always works for the good of those who love Him according to His great purpose!

We covered a lot of ground this week. I pray that God spoke to your heart as we studied the beginning of Saul's journey and then a little more about Peter. I pray that God is preparing you for whatever He has next in your life. Praise Him in the waiting!

What has God spoken to you over this last week in Acts 9?

This coming group time will be the last discussion time. Is there anything you would like to share with the group regarding God's work in your life over these past eight weeks in Acts?

WEEK 8
Commentary: The Miracle of the Cross

This week had a little drama for me—much more excitement than usual. My darling husband was out of town for the week, and he really could not have picked a worse week to go. I had to pick up my son from the airport in Virginia (I live in Maryland) at seven thirty on Saturday morning. Since my son is thirteen, I had to get a security pass and meet him at the gate, which is not something I wanted to do with two small children at six o'clock in the morning. Therefore, an old babysitter planned to stay on Friday night and watch the girls after while I went to get Parker.

On Thursday morning, the babysitter texted me to say that she wasn't able to make it because something came up. I get it. Normally, it wouldn't make any difference, but this time, it really left me in a bind. I started thinking of everyone else I could ask. I sent out texts and ran through all the high school girls at the church. Every single one was either out of town or going on our annual youth beach trip.

I started texting my single girlfriends, but none of them could watch the girls. I started feeling like something was going to happen, and I just kind of shot up a prayer and decided not to stress. Last night, my best friend of over ten years called me out of the blue. It had been months since we chatted—and at least a year since I'd seen her. After some chit chat, I ended up telling her about the bind I was in. She offered to come up on Friday and watch the kids for me! She believed she just randomly called me, but I knew that God had been at work. He pulled some strings, found me a babysitter, and helped me reconnect with my best friend all at the same time. There is no such thing as coincidence when God is involved.

We are going to look at chapter 10 today—the last chapter of this eight-week study. We serve a God who is very much in control of our circumstances. He is not about coincidence; He is about divine opportunity! This chapter is full of God-given events and opportunities.

Turn to the very last verse of chapter 9 and read 9:43 with me.

Peter stayed in Joppa with a tanner named Simon. Jewish tanners were despised as outcasts because they were constantly ceremonially "unclean." Not by chance, Peter's next vision deals with "unclean" humans. Even as we are told with whom Peter is staying, we see that God is preparing Peter for a revelation. God is continuing to stretch Peter's thoughts regarding the meaning of the word "unclean."

Let's read Acts 10:1–8:

> [1] At Caesarea there was a man named Cornelius, a centurion of what was known as the Italian Cohort, [2] a devout man who feared God with all his household, gave alms generously to the people, and prayed continually to God. [3] About the ninth hour of the day[a] he saw clearly in a vision an angel of God come in and say to him, "Cornelius." [4] And he stared at him in terror and said, "What is it, Lord?" And he said to him, "Your prayers and your alms have ascended as a memorial before God. [5] And now send men to Joppa and bring one Simon who is called Peter. [6] He is lodging with one Simon, a tanner, whose house is by the sea." [7] When the angel who spoke to him had departed, he called two of his servants and a devout soldier from among those who attended him, [8] and having related everything to them, he sent them to Joppa.

We are introduced to a Roman centurion from the Italian Cohort. Cornelius is, for all intents and purposes, a policeman. Verse 2 says he is a devout man who feared God, along with all his household, he gave alms generously to the people, and he prayed continually to God. Instead of some centurion who takes advantage of his position, we see him as the epitome of righteous living. He is a Gentile, yet he knows the scripture and follows it by loving God and loving people, just as Jewish law says.

At around three o'clock in the afternoon, the ninth hour of the day, he has a vision of the angel of God. Not coincidentally, this is the exact time of the second daily sacrifice held in the Jewish temple. The angel tells him that God has heard his prayers and accepted his alms as a memorial.

Esler says, "The prayers and alms of this Gentile were accepted to God in lieu of the sacrifices which he was not allowed to enter the temple to offer himself. In other words, God had acted to break down barriers between Jews and Gentiles by treating the prayers and alms of a Gentile as equivalent to the sacrifice of a Jew."[62]

God heard his prayers, saw his sacrifices of alms, and considered him righteous—even as a Gentile. Thus, the angel in the vision tells him to send two men to Joppa to find Peter. The angel leaves and Cornelius immediately gathers two servants and a devout soldier and sends them to find Peter.

This chapter does not go three verses before God is already intervening in Cornelius's life. In the previous chapter, the amount of direct intervention by God showed us how important Saul's conversion was to God. Similarly, this entire chapter is inundated with visions and direct actions by the Holy Spirit. Just like in chapter 9, Luke means to show us that the events that unfold in this chapter are vitally important to the fulfilment of God's plan. God is very clearly the puppeteer throughout this chapter, pulling the strings to bring Cornelius, the Gentile, and Peter, the devout Christian Jew, together.

Please continue reading vv. 9–23:

> [9] The next day, as they were on their journey and approaching the city, Peter went up on the housetop about the sixth hour[b] to pray. [10] And he became hungry and wanted something to eat, but while they were preparing it, he fell into a trance [11] and saw the heavens opened and something like a great sheet descending, being let down by its four corners upon the earth. [12] In it were all kinds of animals and reptiles and birds of the air. [13] And there

---

[62] Philip Esler, *Community and Gospel in Luke-Acts: The Social and Political Motivations of Lucan Theology* (Cambridge: Cambridge University Press, 1987) 162.

came a voice to him: "Rise, Peter; kill and eat." [14] But Peter said, "By no means, Lord; for I have never eaten anything that is common or unclean." [15] And the voice came to him again a second time, "What God has made clean, do not call common." [16] This happened three times, and the thing was taken up at once to heaven.

[17] Now while Peter was inwardly perplexed as to what the vision that he had seen might mean, behold, the men who were sent by Cornelius, having made inquiry for Simon's house, stood at the gate [18] and called out to ask whether Simon who was called Peter was lodging there. [19] And while Peter was pondering the vision, the Spirit said to him, "Behold, three men are looking for you. [20] Rise and go down and accompany them without hesitation,[c] for I have sent them." [21] And Peter went down to the men and said, "I am the one you are looking for. What is the reason for your coming?" [22] And they said, "Cornelius, a centurion, an upright and God-fearing man, who is well spoken of by the whole Jewish nation, was directed by a holy angel to send for you to come to his house and to hear what you have to say." [23] So he invited them in to be his guests.

This vision is fascinating because God does not spell out the meaning for Peter. A huge sheet descends from heaven with all kinds of animals, reptiles, and birds—even the unclean ones. As Peter looks upon the vision, a voice from heaven tells him to rise and eat.

In shock, Peter replies, "By no means!" His horrified response indicates that he thought he was being tested because of all the unclean animals.[63]

In verse 15, the voice replies, "What God has made clean, do not call common."

After this happens three times, the sheet is taken back up to heaven. What is it about Peter and the number three? Jesus asks him if he loves

---

[63] If you're interested, you can find this list in Leviticus 11.

Him three times.[64] Peter denies Jesus three times.[65] Peter is told three times that he may not call common what God has made clean. Maybe Peter needed that number before he really got it in his brain. I think I would be happy if God only needed to tell me three times before I got it!

Peter is reluctant and resistant to the direction in the vision. He knows this vision has a meaning, but he can't figure it out. While he is pondering the vision, the men that God told Cornelius to send show up at Simon the Tanner's house looking for Peter. It was too late for them to set off for Cornelius's house that day, so Peter invites them to stay the night and set off for Caesarea the next day.

Let's look at what happens when he gets there in verses 23b–33:

> The next day he rose and went away with them, and some of the brothers from Joppa accompanied him. [24] And on the following day they entered Caesarea. Cornelius was expecting them and had called together his relatives and close friends. [25] When Peter entered, Cornelius met him and fell down at his feet and worshiped him. [26] But Peter lifted him up, saying, "Stand up; I too am a man." [27] And as he talked with him, he went in and found many persons gathered. [28] And he said to them, "You yourselves know how unlawful it is for a Jew to associate with or to visit anyone of another nation, but God has shown me that I should not call any person common or unclean. [29] So when I was sent for, I came without objection. I ask then why you sent for me."
>
> [30] And Cornelius said, "Four days ago, about this hour, I was praying in my house at the ninth hour,[d] and behold, a man stood before me in bright clothing [31] and said, 'Cornelius, your prayer has been heard and your alms have been remembered before God. [32] Send therefore to Joppa and ask for Simon who is called Peter. He is lodging in the house of Simon, a tanner, by the sea.' [33] So I sent for

---

[64] John 21:15–17.
[65] Luke 22:54–62.

you at once, and you have been kind enough to come. Now therefore we are all here in the presence of God to hear all that you have been commanded by the Lord."

In verse 24, we are told that Cornelius was expecting Peter to arrive and had called together his relatives and close friends. I love this verse. It tells us that Cornelius had no idea what to expect, but he was expecting something momentous! When we see God working hard to bring something together, we too should expect something momentous! You cannot out-expect what God wants to give you. Amen!

As Peter arrives to the house, Cornelius falls to his feet in verse 25. It's such an interesting action because we can see that sometimes even those considered righteous can get it so very wrong. Peter quickly rebukes him and reminds him that God alone deserves his worship. Peter then sees the many Gentiles gathered in Cornelius' house and reminds them of the Jewish social custom to not associate or visit anyone of another nation. This is truly a *social* custom. It is not part of Torah; it was adopted by the customs of the time. Even as he is reminding them of the social custom, he realizes the meaning of the vision: God has shown him that he should not call any person unclean.

Between the time the men found Peter at the tanner's house and this point, Peter finally got it. Christ's sacrifice cleansed all people so that no person could ever again be considered unclean according to Jewish Law.

With this realization in mind, Peter asks why they sent for him. In reply, Cornelius tells him about his vision from God. And then we come to this incredible verse in 33b: "Now therefore we are all here in the presence of God to hear all that you have been commanded by the Lord."

The language in this verse harkens back to Acts 1:13–14 when the apostles were waiting for the Pentecost in the upper room. Many people think that Luke is suggesting that this is the "Gentile Pentecost" that opens the door for the mission to the Gentiles.

Peter opens his mouth and gives the gospel to the Gentiles. Please read verses 34–43:

[34] So Peter opened his mouth and said: "Truly I understand that God shows no partiality, [35] but in every nation anyone

who fears him and does what is right is acceptable to him. [36] As for the word that he sent to Israel, preaching good news of peace through Jesus Christ (he is Lord of all), [37] you yourselves know what happened throughout all Judea, beginning from Galilee after the baptism that John proclaimed: [38] how God anointed Jesus of Nazareth with the Holy Spirit and with power. He went about doing good and healing all who were oppressed by the devil, for God was with him. [39] And we are witnesses of all that he did both in the country of the Jews and in Jerusalem. They put him to death by hanging him on a tree, [40] but God raised him on the third day and made him to appear, [41] not to all the people but to us who had been chosen by God as witnesses, who ate and drank with him after he rose from the dead. [42] And he commanded us to preach to the people and to testify that he is the one appointed by God to be judge of the living and the dead. [43] To him all the prophets bear witness that everyone who believes in him receives forgiveness of sins through his name."

We finally come to the phrase after which this study is named: "God shows no partiality." If you follow God through the Bible, His eternal plan from the very beginning was for every single person on this planet—who ever lived, who are living now, and those who will live in the future—to come to Him. And so it all comes back to Jesus.

The miracle for this week is the miracle of the cross. Everything we have studied has been because of his sacrifice. It is all because of the love that surrounds the cross event. Jesus died on the cross for each of us—for every man, every woman, rich, poor, of ever color, tongue and nationality—so that not one of us could ever again be considered unclean. I am reminded of Zechariah 3:1–4:

Then he showed me Joshua the high priest standing before the angel of the Lord, and Satan standing at his right side to accuse him. [2] The Lord said to Satan, "The Lord rebuke you, Satan! The Lord, who has chosen

Jerusalem, rebuke you! Is not this man a burning stick snatched from the fire?"

³ Now Joshua was dressed in filthy clothes as he stood before the angel. ⁴ The angel said to those who were standing before him, "Take off his filthy clothes."

Then he said to Joshua, "See, I have taken away your sin, and I will put fine garments on you."

This is one of the moments where we get to see Satan in his office as the accuser—the one who is telling God that you deserve nothing but death. We see Joshua dressed in filthy clothes—as we all once were. I love this scene. Do you remember when you appeared before Christ, dressed in your filth, and He said, "Take off your filthy clothes. See, I have taken away your sin, and I will put fine garments upon you."

The cross is everything. It is the reason we are here, it is the reason why we live, and it is the reason why we can have joy and love and life in abundance. Finally, in this last week of study, we end with the chapter that is the beginning of the fulfillment of Jesus's command in Acts 1:8. We end this study at the moment of our beginning: when the cross was finally extended to the Gentile world.

Let's read the rest of chapter 10 and see their reactions:

⁴⁴ While Peter was still saying these things, the Holy Spirit fell on all who heard the word. ⁴⁵ And the believers from among the circumcised who had come with Peter were amazed, because the gift of the Holy Spirit was poured out even on the Gentiles. ⁴⁶ For they were hearing them speaking in tongues and extolling God. Then Peter declared, ⁴⁷ "Can anyone withhold water for baptizing these people, who have received the Holy Spirit just as we have?" ⁴⁸ And he commanded them to be baptized in the name of Jesus Christ. Then they asked him to remain for some days.

"And while Peter was still saying these things." Finally, the spiritual status of the Gentiles reflected their spiritual desires. They had a fierce love for the God of the Jews, and for the first time in the New Testament era, we see that God is offered as the God of the Gentiles. We see the fulfillment of His promises to Abraham, to David.

While the gospel was still being offered, the Gentiles are filled with the Holy Spirit and begin speaking in tongues of ecstatic speech. They praise God with abandon, and they are baptized in the name of Christ.

We began our study with the miracle of Jesus's birth, and we are ending it with the miracle of Jesus's death on the cross and his subsequent resurrection. As Paul said more than twenty years after we meet him in Acts 9, "For if we have been united with [Jesus] in a death like his, we shall certainly be united with him in a resurrection like his" (Romans 6:5). If you have put your faith in Christ, you are dead to your old self of sin and have risen with Christ into a new life of holiness and righteousness—a life filled with the Spirit of God. Praise you, Jesus!

Believe in the power of God to work in your life. Ask outrageously of Him. Have faith that God is able and willing to work miracles in your life, and live in the freedom into which you have been called.

I want to end this journey with the words of Paul to the church of Ephesus in Ephesians 1:16-23:

> [16] I do not cease to give thanks for you, remembering you in my prayers, [17] that the God of our Lord Jesus Christ, the Father of glory, may give you the Spirit of wisdom and of revelation in the knowledge of him, [18] having the eyes of your hearts enlightened, that you may know what is the hope to which he has called you, what are the riches of his glorious inheritance in the saints, [19] and what is the immeasurable greatness of his power toward us who believe, according to the working of his great might [20] that he worked in Christ when he raised him from the dead and seated him at his right hand in the heavenly places, [21] far above all rule and authority and power and dominion, and above every name that is named, not only in this age but also in the one to come. [22] And he put all things under his feet and gave him as head over all things to the church, [23] which is his body, the fullness of him who fills all in all.

185

It has been my sincere honor to have taken this journey with you. I thank you for persevering through it and I pray that God is blessing your efforts many times over.

With so much love and so many blessings, Audrey.

APPENDIX 1
Prophecies Christ Fulfilled

	Prophecies about Jesus	Prophecy Made	Prophecy Fulfilled
1	Messiah would be a descendant of Abraham.	Genesis 12:13; 22:18	Matthew 1:1
2	Messiah would be a descendant of Isaac.	Genesis 17:19; 21:12	Luke 3:34
3	Messiah would be a descendant of Jacob.	Numbers 24:17	Matthew 1:2
4	Messiah would come from the tribe of Judah.	Genesis 49:10	Luke 3:33
5	Messiah would be heir to King David's throne.	2 Samuel 7:12–13	Luke 1:32–33
6	Messiah would be preceded by Elijah.	Malachi 4:5–6	Matthew 11:13–14
7	A messenger would prepare the way for the Messiah.	Isaiah 40:3–5	Luke 3:3–6
8	Messiah would be born of a virgin.	Isaiah 7:14	Matthew 1:22–23; Luke 1:26–31
9	Messiah would be called Immanuel.	Isaiah 7:14	Matthew 1:23
10	Messiah would be born in Bethlehem.	Micah 5:2	Matthew 2:1; Luke 2:4–6

	Prophecies about Jesus	Prophecy Made	Prophecy Fulfilled
11	Messiah would spend time in Egypt.	Hosea 11:1	Matthew 2:14–15
12	A massacre of children would happen in the place the Messiah was born.	Jeremiah 31:15	Matthew 2:16–18
13	Messiah would be called a Nazarene.	Isaiah 11:1	Matthew 2:23
14	Messiah would be declared the Son of God.	Psalm 2:7	Matthew 3:16–17
15	Messiah would bring light to Galilee.	Isaiah 9:1–2	Matthew 4:13–16
16	Messiah would be a prophet.	Deuteronomy 18:15	Acts 3:20–22
17	Messiah would speak in parables.	Isaiah 6:9–10	Matthew 13:10–15, 34–35
18	Messiah would be sent to heal the brokenhearted.	Isaiah 61:1–2	Luke 4:18–19
19	Messiah would be praised by little children.	Psalm 8:2	Matthew 21:16
20	Messiah would be rejected by his own people.	Isaiah 53:3	John 1:11
21	Messiah would be betrayed.	Zechariah 11:12–13	Matthew 26:14–16; Luke 22:47–48
22	Messiah's price money would be used to buy a potter's field.	Zechariah 11:12–13	Matthew 27:9–10
23	Messiah would be falsely accused.	Psalm 35:11	Mark 14:57–58
24	Messiah would be silent before his accusers.	Isaiah 53:7	Mark 15:4–5
25	Messiah would be spat upon and struck.	Isaiah 50:6	Matthew 26:67

	Prophecies about Jesus	Prophecy Made	Prophecy Fulfilled
26	Messiah would be called King.	Zechariah 9:9	Matthew 27:37; Mark 11:7–11
27	Messiah would be hated without cause	Psalms 35:19; 69:4	John 15:24–25
28	Messiah would be given vinegar to drink.	Psalm 69:21	Matthew 27:34; John 19:28–30
29	Messiah would be crucified with criminals.	Isaiah 53:12	Matthew 27:38; Mark 15:27–28
30	Messiah's hands and feet would be pierced.	Zechariah 12:10	John 20:25–27
31	Soldiers would gamble for Messiah's garments.	Psalm 22:18	Matthew 27:35–36; Luke 23:34
32	Messiah would be mocked and ridiculed.	Psalm 22:7–8	Luke 23:35
33	Messiah would pray for his enemies.	Psalm 109:4	Luke 23:34
34	Messiah would be forsaken by God.	Psalm 22:18	Matthew 27:46
35	Messiah's bones would not be broken.	Psalm 34:20	John 19:33–36
36	Soldiers would pierce the Messiah's side.	Zechariah 12:10	John 19:34
37	Messiah would be buried with the rich.	Isaiah 53:9	Matthew 27:57–60
38	Messiah would resurrect from the dead.	Psalms 16:10; 49:15	Matthew 28:2–7; Acts 2:22–32
39	Messiah would ascend to heaven.	Psalm 24:7–10	Mark 16:19; Luke 24:41
40	Messiah would be seated at God's right hand.	Psalm 68:18; 110:1	Mark 16:19; Matthew 22:44

	Prophecies about Jesus	Prophecy Made	Prophecy Fulfilled
41	Messiah would be a sacrifice for sin.	Isaiah 53:5–12	Romans 5:6–8
42	Messiah's throne will be anointed and eternal.	Psalm 45:6–7; Daniel 2:44	Luke 1:33; Hebrews 1:8–12

APPENDIX 2
The Holy Spirit ...

Invites us to Christ

- The Spirit and the Bride say, "Come." And let the one who hears say, "Come." And let the one who is thirsty come; let the one who desires take the water of life without price. (Revelation 22:17)

Seals us in salvation

- And do not grieve the Holy Spirit of God, by whom you were sealed for the day of redemption. (Ephesians 4:30)

- And it is God who establishes us with you in Christ, and has anointed us, and who has also put his seal on us and given us his Spirit in our hearts as a guarantee. (2 Corinthians 1:21–22)

Fellowships with us

- The Holy Spirit is God who makes his tabernacle in us; we are not on our own; you were bought at a price. (1 Corinthians 6:19–20)

- The grace of the Lord Jesus Christ and the love of God and the fellowship of the Holy Spirit be with you all. (2 Corinthians 13:14)

- You however, are not in the flesh but in the Spirit, if in fact the Spirit of God dwells in you. (Romans 8:9)

- Hope does not put us to shame, because God's love has been poured into our hearts through the Holy Spirit who has been given to us. (Romans 5:5)

Renews and transforms us

- He saved us, not because of works done by us in righteousness, but according to his own mercy, by the washing of regeneration and renewal of the Holy Spirit. (Titus 3:5)

- But the fruit of the Spirit is love, joy, peace, patience, kindness, goodness, faithfulness, gentleness, self-control; against such things there is no law. (Galatians 5:22–23)

- And we all, with unveiled faces, beholding the glory of the Lord, are being transformed into the same image from one degree of glory to another. (2 Corinthians 3:18)

Gives us peace

- Peace I leave with you; my peace I give to you. Not as the world gives do I give to you. Let not your hearts be troubled, neither let them be afraid. (John 14:27)

- For to set the mind on the flesh is death, but to set the mind on the Spirit is life and peace. (Romans 8:6)

- For the kingdom of God is not a matter of eating and drinking but of righteousness and peace and joy in the Holy Spirit. (Romans 14:17)

Guides us

- Then Jesus was led up by the Spirit into the wilderness to be tempted by the devil. (Matthew 4:1)

- But I say, walk by the Spirit, and you will not gratify the desires of the flesh. (Galatians 5:16)

- I am speaking the truth in Christ—I am not lying; my conscience bears me witness in the Holy Spirit. (Romans 9:1)

- When the Spirit of Truth comes, he will guide you in all the truth. (John 16:13)

- And I will give you a new heart, and a new Spirit I will put within you. And I will remove the heart of stone from your flesh and give you a heart of flesh. And I will put my Spirit within you, and cause you to walk in my statues and be careful to obey my rules. (Ezekiel 36:26–27)

- And we impart this in words not taught by human wisdom by taught by the Spirit, interpreting spiritual truths to those who are spiritual. (1 Corinthians 2:13)

Helps us

- And I will ask the Father, and he will give you another Helper, to be with you forever, even the Spirit of truth, whom the world cannot receive, because it neither sees him nor knows him. (John 14:16–17)

- But the Helper, the Holy Spirit, whom the Father will send in my name, he will teach you all things and bring to your remembrance all that I have said to you. (John 14:26)

- Likewise the Spirit helps us in our weakness. For we do not know what to pray for as we ought, but the Spirit himself intercedes for us with groanings too deep for words. (Romans 8:26)

Empowers us

- But you will receive power when the Holy Spirit has come upon you, and you will be my witnesses in Jerusalem and in all Judea and Samaria, and to the end of the earth. (Acts 1:8)

- Now there are varieties of gifts, but the same Spirit; and there are varieties of service, but the same Lord; and there are varieties of activities, but it is the same God who empowers them all in everyone. (1 Corinthians 12:4–6)

APPENDIX 3
Scriptures of Healing

Then they cried to the Lord in their trouble, and he saved them from their distress. He sent forth his word and healed them; he rescued them from the grave. Let them give thanks to the Lord for his unfailing love and his wonderful deeds for men. (Psalm 107:19–21)

The people living in darkness have seen a great light; on those living in the land of the Shadow of Death, a light has dawned. (Isaiah 9:2)

O Lord my God, I called to you for help and you healed me. (Psalm 30:2)

Surely he took up our infirmities and carried our sorrows, yet we considered him stricken by God, smitten by him, and afflicted. But he was pierced for our transgressions, he was crushed for our iniquities; the punishment that brought us peace was upon him, and by his wounds we are healed. (Isaiah 53:4–5)

Praise the Lord, O my soul, and forget not all his benefits—who forgives all your sins and heals all your diseases, who redeems your life from the pit and crowns you with love and compassion. (Psalm 103:2–4)

Fear not, for I am with you; be not dismayed, for I am your God; I will strengthen you, I will help you, I will uphold you with my righteous right hand. (Isaiah 41:10)

Come to me, all who labor and are heavy laden, and I will give you rest. Take my yoke upon you, and learn from me, for I am gentle and lowly in heart, and you will find rest for your souls. For my yoke is easy, and my burden is light. (Matthew 11:28–30)

He heals the brokenhearted and binds up their wounds. (Psalm 147:3)

Before they call, I will answer; while they are yet speaking, I will hear. (Isaiah 65:24)

Heal me, O Lord, and I will be healed; save me and I will be saved, for you are the one I praise. (Jeremiah 17:14)

Let us then approach the throne of grace with confidence, so that we may receive mercy and find grace to help us in our time of need. (Hebrews 4:16)

He will wipe every tear from their eyes. There will be no more death or mourning or crying or pain, for the old order of things has passed away. (Revelation 21:4)

APPENDIX 4
Set Free

For I will forgive their wickedness and will remember their sins no more. (Hebrews 8:12)

Surely it was for my benefit that I suffered such anguish. In your love you kept me from the pit of destruction; you have put all my sins behind your back. (Isaiah 38:17)

I, even I, am he who blots out your transgressions, for my own sake, and remembers your sins no more. (Isaiah 43:25)

"No longer will they teach their neighbor, or say to one another, 'Know the LORD,' because they will all know me, from the least of them to the greatest," declares the LORD. "For I will forgive their wickedness and will remember their sins no more." (Jeremiah 31:34)

I will cleanse them from all the sin they have committed against me and will forgive all their sins of rebellion against me. (Jeremiah 33:8)

The angel said to those who were standing before him, "Take off his filthy clothes." Then he said to Joshua, "See, I have taken away your sin, and I will put fine garments on you." (Zechariah 3:4)

Now the Lord is the Spirit, and where the Spirit of the Lord is, there is freedom. (2 Corinthians 3:17)

There is therefore now no condemnation for those who are in Christ Jesus. For the law of the Spirit of life has set you free in Christ Jesus from the law of sin and death. (Romans 8:1–2)

He will again have compassion on us; he will tread our iniquities underfoot. You will cast all our sins into the depths of the sea. (Micah 7:19)

Now the Lord is the Spirit, and where the Spirit of the Lord is, there is freedom! (Corinthians 3:17)

So if the Son sets you free, you will be free indeed! (John 8:36)

It is for freedom that Christ has set us free. Stand firm, then, and do not let yourselves be burdened again by a yoke of slavery. (Galatians 5:1)

In my anguish I cried to the LORD, and he answered by setting me free. (Psalm 118:5)

Delivered

The LORD is my rock, my fortress and my deliverer. 2 Sam 22:2

The LORD replied, "Don't say, 'I'm too young,' for you must go wherever I send you and say whatever I tell you. And don't be afraid of the people, for I will be with you and will protect you. I, the LORD, have spoken!" (Jeremiah 1:7–8)

I sought the LORD, and he answered me; he delivered me from all my fears. (Psalm 34:4)

He lifted me out of the slimy pit, out of the mud and mire; he set my feet on a rock and gave me a firm place to stand. (Psalm 40:2)

He sent out his word and healed them; he rescued them from the grave. (Psalm 107:20)

The righteous cry out, and the LORD hears them; he delivers them from all their troubles. (Psalm 34:17)

Then they cried out to the LORD in their trouble, and he delivered them from their distress. (Psalm 107:6)

This shows that the Lord knows how to rescue godly people from their sufferings and to punish evil people while they wait for the Day of Judgment. (2 Peter 2:9)

Yes, I am the gate. Those who come in through me will be saved. They will come and go freely and will find good pastures. The thief's purpose is to steal and kill and destroy. My purpose is to give them a rich and satisfying life. I am the good shepherd. The good shepherd sacrifices his life for the sheep. (John 10:9–11)

Israel, you will know that I stand at your side. I am the LORD your God—there are no other gods. Never again will you be put to shame. (Joel 2:27)

You, Lord, took up my case; you redeemed my life. (Lamentations 3:58)

And call on me in the day of trouble; I will deliver you, and you will honor me. (Psalm 50:15)

You will not have to fight this battle. Take up your positions; stand firm and see the deliverance the LORD will give you, O Judah and Jerusalem. Do not be afraid; do not be discouraged. Go out to face them tomorrow, and the LORD will be with you. (2 Chronicles 20:17)

From the LORD comes deliverance. May your blessing be on your people. (Psalm 3:8)

APPENDIX 5
You are Chosen

Before I formed you in the womb I knew you, and before you were born I consecrated you; I appointed you a prophet to the nations. (Jeremiah 1:5)

For you are a people holy to the LORD your God. The LORD your God has chosen you to be a people for his treasured possession, out of all the peoples who are on the face of the earth. (Deuteronomy 7:6)

But now thus says the Lord, he who created you, O Jacob, he who formed you, O Israel: "Fear not, for I have redeemed you; I have called you by name, you are mine. When you pass through the waters, I will be with you; and through the rivers, they shall not overwhelm you; when you walk through fire you shall not be burned, and the flame shall not consume you. For I am the Lord your God, the Holy One of Israel, your Savior. (Isaiah 43:1–3)

And we know that for those who love God all things work together for good, for those who are called according to his purpose. For those whom he foreknew he also predestined to be conformed to the image of his Son, in order that he might be the firstborn among many brothers. And those whom he predestined he also called, and those whom he called he also justified, and those whom he justified he also glorified. (Romans 8:28–30)

He chose us in him before the foundation of the world, that we should be holy and blameless before him. In love he predestined us for adoption as sons through Jesus Christ, according to the purpose of his will, to the praise of his glorious grace, with which he has blessed us in the beloved. (Ephesians 1:4–6)

For we know, brothers loved by God, that he has chosen you. (1 Thessalonians 1:4)

But we ought always to give thanks to God for you, brothers beloved by the Lord, because God chose you as the firstfruits to be saved, through sanctification by the Spirit and belief in the truth. (2 Thessalonians 2:13)

For a Purpose

But for this purpose I have raised you up, to show you my power, so that my name may be proclaimed in all the earth. (Exodus 9:16)

For I know the plans I have for you, declares the LORD, plans for welfare and not for evil, to give you a future and a hope. (Jeremiah 29:11)

I am the LORD; I HAVE CALLED YOU IN RIGHTEOUSNESS; I WILL TAKE YOU BY THE HAND AND KEEP YOU; I will give you as a covenant for the people, a light for the nations. (Isaiah 42:6)

You did not choose me, but I chose you and appointed you that you should go and bear fruit and that your fruit should abide, so that whatever you ask the Father in my name, he may give it to you. (John 15:16)

In him we have obtained an inheritance, having been predestined according to the purpose of him who works all things according to the counsel of his will, so that we who were the first to hope in Christ might be to the praise of his glory. (Ephesians 1:11–12)

For we are his workmanship, created in Christ Jesus for good works, which God prepared beforehand, that we should walk in them. (Ephesians 2:10)

So, whether you eat or drink, or whatever you do, do all to the glory of God. (1 Corinthians 10:31)

As each has received a gift, use it to serve one another, as good stewards of God's varied grace: whoever speaks, as one who speaks oracles of God; whoever serves, as one who serves by the strength that God supplies—in order that in everything God may be glorified through Jesus Christ. (1 Peter 4:10–11)

But you are a chosen people, a royal priesthood, a holy nation, God's special possession, that you may declare the praises of him who called you out of darkness into his wonderful light. (1 Peter 2:9)

APPENDIX 6
Unveiled Faces

Moreover, I will give you a new heart and put a new spirit within you; and I will remove the heart of stone from your flesh and give you a heart of flesh. (Ezekiel 36:26)

And do not be conformed to this world, but be transformed by the renewing of your mind, so that you may prove what the will of God is, that which is good and acceptable and perfect. (Romans 12:2)

Therefore if anyone is in Christ, he is a new creature; the old things passed away; behold, new things have come. (2 Corinthians 5:17)

In reference to your former manner of life, you lay aside the old self, which is being corrupted in accordance with the lusts of deceit, and that you be renewed in the spirit of your mind, and put on the new self, which in the likeness of God has been created in righteousness and holiness of the truth. (Ephesians 4:22–24)

And although you were formerly alienated and hostile in mind, engaged in evil deeds, yet He has now reconciled you in His fleshly body through death, in order to present you before Him holy and blameless and beyond reproach. (Colossians 1:21–22)

He saved us, not on the basis of deeds which we have done in righteousness, but according to His mercy, by the washing of regeneration and renewing by the Holy Spirit. (Titus 3:5)

Beloved, we are God's children now, and what we will be has not yet appeared; but we know that when he appears we shall be like him, because we shall see him as he is. And everyone who thus hopes in him purifies himself as he is pure. (1 John 3:2–3)

And we all, with unveiled face, beholding the glory of the Lord, are being transformed into the same image from one degree of glory to another. For this comes from the Lord who is the Spirit. (2 Corinthians 3:18)

APPENDIX 7
The Throne of Grace

For by works of the law no human being will be justified in his sight, since through the law comes knowledge of sin. But now the righteousness of God has been manifested apart from the law, although the Law and the Prophets bear witness to it — the righteousness of God through faith in Jesus Christ for all who believe. For there is no distinction: for all have sinned and fall short of the glory of God, and are justified by his grace as a gift, through the redemption that is in Christ Jesus. (Romans 3:20–24)

Therefore, since we have been justified by faith, we have peace with God through our Lord Jesus Christ. Through him we have also obtained access by faith into this grace in which we stand, and we rejoice in hope of the glory of God. (Romans 5:1–2)

Therefore, as one trespass led to condemnation for all men, so one act of righteousness leads to justification and life for all men. For as by the one man's disobedience the many were made sinners, so by the one man's obedience the many will be made righteous. Now the law came in to increase the trespass, but where sin increased, grace abounded all the more, so that, as sin reigned in death, grace also might reign through righteousness leading to eternal life through Jesus Christ our Lord. (Romans 5:18–21)

Having gifts that differ according to the grace given to us, let us use them: if prophecy, in proportion to our faith; if service, in our serving; the one who teaches, in his teaching; the one who exhorts, in his exhortation; the one who contributes, in generosity; the one who leads, with zeal; the one who does acts of mercy, with cheerfulness. (Romans 12:6–8)

For by grace you have been saved through faith. And this is not your own doing; it is the gift of God. (Ephesians 2:8)

For the grace of God has appeared, bringing salvation for all people, training us to renounce ungodliness and worldly passions, and to live self-controlled, upright, and godly lives in the present age, waiting for our blessed hope, the appearing of the glory of our great God and Savior Jesus Christ, who gave himself for us to redeem us from all lawlessness and to purify for himself a people for his own possession who are zealous for good works. (Titus 2:11–14)

Let us then with confidence draw near to the throne of grace, that we may receive mercy and find grace to help in time of need. (Hebrews 4:16)

As each has received a gift, use it to serve one another, as good stewards of God's varied grace: whoever speaks, as one who speaks oracles of God; whoever serves, as one who serves by the strength that God supplies—in order that in everything God may be glorified through Jesus Christ. (1 Peter 4:10–11)

And after you have suffered a little while, the God of all grace, who has called you to his eternal glory in Christ, will himself restore, confirm, strengthen, and establish you. (1 Peter 5:10)

APPENDIX 8
Crucified with Christ

For Christ also suffered once for sins, the righteous for the unrighteous, that he might bring us to God, being put to death in the flesh but made alive in the spirit. (1 Peter 3:18)

Therefore, since we are surrounded by so great a cloud of witnesses, let us also lay aside every weight, and sin which clings so closely, and let us run with endurance the race that is set before us, looking to Jesus, the founder and perfecter of our faith, who for the joy that was set before him endured the cross, despising the shame, and is seated at the right hand of the throne of God. (Hebrews 12:1–2)

For the word of the cross is folly to those who are perishing, but to us who are being saved it is the power of God. (1 Corinthians 1:18)

We know that our old self was crucified with him in order that the body of sin might be brought to nothing, so that we would no longer be enslaved to sin. (Romans 6:6)

For it was the Father's good pleasure for all the fullness to dwell in Him, and through Him to reconcile all things to Himself, having made peace through the blood of His cross; through Him, I say, whether things on earth or things in heaven. (Colossians 1:19–20)

He made you alive together with Him, having forgiven us all our transgressions, having canceled out the certificate of debt consisting of decrees against us, which was hostile to us; and He has taken it out of the way, having nailed it to the cross. (Colossians 2:13b–14)

For he himself is our peace, who has made us both one and has broken down in his flesh the dividing wall of hostility by abolishing the law of commandments expressed in ordinances, that he might create in himself one new man in place of the two, so making peace, and might reconcile us both to God in one body through the cross, thereby killing the hostility. (Ephesians 2:14–16)

I have been crucified with Christ. It is no longer I who live, but Christ who lives in me. And the life I now live in the flesh I live by faith in the Son of God, who loved me and gave himself for me. (Galatians 2:20)

But God demonstrates His own love toward us, in that while we were yet sinners, Christ died for us. (Romans 5:8)

For God so loved the world, that He gave His only begotten Son, that whoever believes in Him shall not perish, but have eternal life. For God did not send the Son into the world to judge the world, but that the world might be saved through Him. (John 3:16–17)

Therefore if any man be in Christ, he is a new creature: old things are passed away; behold, all things are become new. (2 Corinthians 5:17)

We were buried therefore with him by baptism into death, in order that, just as Christ was raised from the dead by the glory of the Father, we too might walk in newness of life. (Romans 6:4)

Works Cited

Barrett, C. K. *Acts*. Vol. 1. International Critical Commentary. MPG Books, 2002.

Easton, Matthew George. "Calling." Bible Study Tools. 2014. Accessed August 9, 2016. http://www.biblestudytools.com/dictionaries/eastons-bible-dictionary/calling.html.

Esler, Philip Francis. *Community and Gospel in Luke-Acts: The Social and Political Motivations of Lucan Theology*. Cambridge: Cambridge University Press, 1987.

Gempf, Conrad. "Acts." In *New Bible Commentary*, 1066-1107. 21st Century ed. Downers Grove, IL: InterVarsity Press, 1994.

Guinness, Os. *The Call: Finding and Fulfilling the Central Purpose of Your Life*. Nashville: Word Publishing, 1998.

Jillette, Penn. "A Gift Of A Bible." YouTube. July 08, 2010. Accessed August 8, 2016. http://youtu.be/6md638smQd8.

Kitz, Anne Marie. "The Hebrew Terminology of Lot Casting and Its Ancient Near Eastern Context." *Catholic Biblical Quarterly* 62, no. 2 (April 2000): 209. Accessed May 20, 2015. ATLA Religion Database [EBSCO].

Lenowitz, Harris. *The Jewish Messiahs: From the Galilee to Crown Heights.* New York: Oxford University Press, 1998.

Muller, George. *The Autobiography of George Muller.* New Kensington, PA: Whitaker House, 1985.

Willimon, William H. "Acts." In *Interpretation Bible Commentary.* Louisville, KY: John Knox Press, 1988.

Witherington, Ben. *The Acts of the Apostles: A Socio-rhetorical Commentary.* Grand Rapids, MI: W.B. Eerdmans Pub., 1998.

About the Author

Audrey Lupisella has a master's in theological studies with a concentration in biblical studies. She has written many devotionals, preached exegetical Bible series, and now focuses on writing Bible studies. She lives with her husband and three children in western Maryland.

Made in the USA
Lexington, KY
04 January 2017